I AM All You Need

Discovering the God Who Is More Than Enough

Mark Chao

I AM All You Need

Discovering the God Who Is More Than Enough

*A*dvantage
BOOKS

Mark Chao

Edited by Jessica Glasner and Allison Morris

Library of Congress Catalog Number: APPLIED FOR

Name:	Chao, Mark, Author
Title:	I AM All You Need by Mark Chao
	Advantage Books, 2025
Identifiers:	ISBN: Paperback: 9781597558532,
	eBook: 9781597558679
Subjects:	RELIGION: Christian Life – Inspirational

First Printing: November 2025
25 26 27 28 29 30   10 9 8 7 6 5 4 3 2 1

Table of Contents

Mark Chao

Foreword

A number of years ago, Bill Rehwald, my adult Sunday school teacher and elder at our then church, Church at Rocky Peak, agreed to disciple me. I had recently recommitted my life to Christ and felt the need to have someone guide me in my walk. We met for breakfast every Monday at 6:30AM at Coco's in Woodland Hills for almost three years.

I am so thankful to Bill for the time he spent with me. One of the first books that Bill and I read through together was *The Knowledge of the Holy* by A. W. Tozer. Bill knew that if I was to get to know God on a personal level, I would need to know who He is, the attributes that He has made known to us through Scripture, and how they are linked together. He wanted to make sure I had an accurate view of God, not skewed by the world or my own baggage.

Tozer was a deep spiritual thinker and a brilliant man. Next to the Bible, *The Knowledge of the Holy* has had the biggest impact on my life and relationship with God. As I read through Tozer's book, I found myself trusting God in a way I never had before and worshipping Him in a new way.

In the midst of my time with Bill, I was forced to resign as a partner from a professional services firm I had been with for 16 years. This was a difficult time, and to complicate matters even more, our beautiful baby girl (Sara) had only been born one month before. With two young children and no job on the horizon, I should have been filled with anxiety. Yet, as I went through this ordeal, I felt God's peace because I knew that God was and is good. The reason I knew He was good is that I was learning God's attributes: that He loves me and that He is faithful. I also knew that He would not break a promise.

Early one morning during my quiet time, as I was going through this career change, I was reading through Philippians, and I got to Philippians 4:6-7, "Do not be anxious about anything, instead bring your petitions to God with thanksgiving and the peace of God, which surpasses all understanding, will guard your hearts and minds in Christ Jesus."[1] These verses contained an action item and a promise. I undertook the action and lifted up my concerns while thanking God. The rest was up to Him. God kept His promise. I felt an incredible peace that was truly beyond all understanding.

How does one feel at peace when he has just lost a job and added another member to the family? (One that, I might add, stole my heart.) Only by God's grace! The peace I felt was a peace that, under the circumstances, did not make any sense but for God's promise. Without Him, this peace would not have been possible.

My incredible wife, Michelle, shared Psalm 32:8 with me during this time, "I will instruct you and teach you in the way you should go; I will counsel you and watch over you." Once more, I watched as God fulfilled His promise in this verse. God had a different plan for me. He realigned my priorities and blessed me with a new job, a better work environment, and more time with my family. All these blessings didn't seem possible at the time until I understood God's character.

Our worldview and our understanding of God impacts our actions and our words. More importantly, it impacts our relationship with Him. In the words of Tozer, "What comes into our minds when we think about God is the most important thing about us."[2]

Think about your deepest relationships. They are deep because you have taken the time to get to know that person. For us to develop a deep relationship with someone typically takes years and years. Over time, we get to know a person's character. They reveal what's important to them. We learn their traits and how they will respond in different situations. We see their sense of humor, their hopes, what makes them tick, their likes and dislikes, and their character. Our

---

[1] ESV.

[2] A.W. Tozer, *The Knowledge of the Holy* (New York: HarperCollins, 1978), 1.

relationship with God is the same. The more we can get to know Him, the deeper our relationship with Him will be.

An incorrect view of God will absolutely impact your relationship with Him. Tozer writes, "I believe there is scarcely an error in doctrine or failure in applying Christian ethics that cannot be traced finally to imperfect and ignoble thoughts about God."[3] There are a number of misconceptions about God that, if you believe to be true, will impact how you interact with Him. Some of these misconceptions are that God is angry, that He is distant or doesn't care, that He is inept, that He is not pure and holy, and for many, that He doesn't exist. Maybe you feel betrayed by Him or that He carries heavy judgement.

If you believe God is angry, you will likely do your best to avoid Him for fear of making Him mad. If you believe He is distant or doesn't care, you will likely not pursue a relationship with Him as it would not be reciprocated. If you believe He is inept, you will likely not turn to Him or trust Him because He's incapable of helping you. If you believe He is not pure and holy, you will likely have no issue with sinning. Finally, if you believe He doesn't exist, well, there would be no reason for a relationship.

In retrospect, the knowledge I had about God helped me to experience His peace when I lost my job. Of course, because God is God, we will never fully know Him. However, there are some things we can know about Him that help guide us into a right relationship with God. I want to share a Biblical view of God to new believers and those seeking to know God better. In this journey of getting to know God and His attributes, my hope is that you will grow closer to Him and realize that the great I AM, is all you need to live a joyful and eternal life that glorifies God.

---

[3] A.W. Tozer, *The Knowledge of the Holy* (New York: HarperCollins, 1978), 1.

Mark Chao

Introduction

I AM

God said to Moses, "I AM WHO I AM. This is what you are to say to the Israelites: 'I AM has sent me to you.'" (Exodus 3:14)

"I tell you the truth," Jesus answered, "before Abraham was born, I am!" (John 8:58)

It's critical to note that I believe the Bible is the inerrant Word of God, and that is reflected in this book. Although it is beyond the scope of this book, the Bible has proven to be historically accurate and continues to be proven true as new discoveries are made despite many efforts to discredit the Bible. It might help you to know that the Bible consists of 66 different books and was written over a period of 1500 years by approximately 40 different authors. Yet, the God of the Bible is described consistently throughout and without contradiction. The God I write about is the God of the Bible.

God's chosen name for Himself is I AM. These two words provide insight into God and who He is. When we make a statement that starts with "I am," we need to add a word or phrase to the end of it. I am happy. I am sad. I am hungry. I am your father. I am going for a bike ride. "I am" in and of itself is typically not sufficient to communicate a complete thought. It needs to be modified by something. But God only uses these two words because He, in and of Himself, is sufficient. No modifiers are necessary. God did not and does not need anyone or anything.

The Book of Exodus tells about how God freed the Israelites from the Egyptians. In the third chapter of Exodus, Moses encounters God in the form of a burning bush. God tells Moses he is to go to Pharaoh (the emperor of the

Egyptians) to bring the Israelites out of Egypt. Moses, being a bit reluctant and unsure, asks God who he should say sent him to free the Israelites, and God responds, "I AM WHO I AM. This is what you are to say to the Israelites: 'I AM sent me to you.'"

In the Book of John, Chapter 8 Jesus encounters Jewish leaders. These leaders are challenging Jesus and they ask Him who He thinks He is. Jesus responds, "before Abraham was born, I am!" He didn't say, "I was." These two words are so simple, yet when they are used to reference God, they are incredibly complex *because they describe God*. There should be no doubt that Jesus was referring to Himself as God as the next verse says that they picked up stones to stone Him as Jesus' claim to being God was blasphemous in their eyes.

The words in this book are intended to help you get to know the Lord better, trust Him more and discover that "I Am" is truly all you need. Psalm 46:10 says, "Be still and know that I am God." It is my hope and prayer that as you read, you will take the time to be still and let your mind ponder the many facets of God and how they intertwine. With that in mind, one question I ask you to consider after you reach the end of *I AM All You Need* is whether there could be a better god than the God of the Bible.

Father God, it is not by accident that this book is in the hands of one of your beloved children. I pray that somehow through my inadequate words, you, the reader, would come to know Him better, trust Him more, and grow in your love for God and others.

In Jesus' name, I pray. Amen.

1

GOD HAS NEVER
AND
WILL NEVER CHANGE

"Jesus Christ is the same yesterday and today and forever." (Hebrews 13:8)

"Every good and perfect gift is from above, coming down from the Father of the heavenly lights, who does not change like shifting shadows." (James 1:17)

"I, the Lord, do not change. So you, O descendants of Jacob, are not destroyed." (Malachi 3:6, ESV)

We often hear the phrase "change is constant." In the business world, operating models and strategies are constantly evolving. If companies don't change, they may be left behind, and worse yet, they may not survive. The internet and Amazon have changed the retail dynamic so significantly that we have seen many brick-and-mortar retailers filing for bankruptcy. Apple changed the cell phone industry and drove a number of competitors into survival mode or out of business (think of flip phone manufacturers and Blackberry). Artificial intelligence has created change at a pace previously unseen.

In the world of athletics, competitors are looking to constantly improve, to innovate. In the world of research, scientists are looking to make that next discovery. In the culinary world, chefs are looking to develop that next award-winning dish. Things are either changing for the better or degrading over time. The young physically grow up and get stronger. The old (including me) start to shrink and become weaker. The young gain knowledge, and the old naturally become more forgetful. You get the picture. Pulling from my high-school days, the word "entropy" comes to mind. Merriam-Webster defines entropy as the degradation of the matter and energy in the universe to an ultimate state of inert uniformity.[1] To put it simply, the universe is constantly changing as it expands, while at the same time, stars die. The world is in a constant state of change, with one exception.

God cannot and will not change.[2] He is the same yesterday and today and forever. Why? Because God is perfect. Something "perfect" is excellent or complete beyond practical or theoretical improvement.[3] Something that is perfect is complete and cannot be improved upon. I submit that if God could get better or change, He would not be God since He would not be perfect. The God Christians and I believe in is so perfect that we can't fully comprehend Him. God's perfection is not because he can't be improved from a "practical" perspective, as the definition suggests. Rather, it's that He can't be improved upon, *period*.

You may be questioning my assertion that God is perfect and that is a fair question. Having said that, here are two Bible verses that tell us God is perfect. 2 Samuel 22:31 says "As for God, his way is perfect; the word of the Lord is flawless." Matthew 5:48 tells us "Be perfect, therefore, as your heavenly Father is perfect." Regardless, please keep this question in mind as you take this journey to learn about God and His character.

One example of God's unchanging nature that overlaps one of His character traits is His *omniscience*. God is omniscient; in other words, He knows all. We will cover this character trait later in the book. If God were not all-knowing, that would indicate that there is more He could learn. The mere act of learning

---

[1] "Entropy." Merriam-Webster.com Dictionary, Merriam-Webster, https://www.merriam-webster.com/dictionary/entropy, accessed December 8, 2022.

[2] See Malachi 3:6 and Hebrews 13:8.

[3] "Perfect." Dictionary.com Dictionary, Dictionary.com, https://www.dictionary.com/browse/perfect#:~:text=entirely%20without%20any%20flaws%2C%20defects,pure%20or%20unmixed%3A%20perfect%20yellow, accessed December 8, 2022.

something that you didn't know before, by definition, changes you. You were not exactly the same as you were before you gained new knowledge. Since God is all-knowing, His level of knowledge can't change. He can't learn more. If God could learn more, He would not be perfect.

How many times have we personally experienced or heard of a married couple that was struggling because he or she wouldn't change? In that sense, we think of change as something positive, something that will improve the relationship. When it comes to our relationship with God, He can't change for the better because He is already good. Furthermore, we wouldn't want Him to change. If He should change, He wouldn't be God.

With this in mind, if we want to improve our relationship with God, the change must come from our end. God gave us many wonderful examples of ways to improve our relationship with Him, particularly through Jesus. Might the change be to spend more time with God in prayer and in the Word? To be more generous? To be humbler? To be more thankful or joyful? To be bolder in Him? To be more loving? We could go on and on, but the point here is that deepening our relationship with God requires *us* to change, not Him.

God's unchanging nature has other implications. My wife, Michelle, and I are blessed with two wonderful children who are now adults. One of the areas I struggled with in raising our children was consistency. We believed consistency was best for our children, as it would give them a sense of security and a clear set of expectations on how to behave. The problem was that I wasn't always consistent with how I handled difficult situations. I remember coming home from a long day of work and finding out one of our children had been disobedient or disrespectful to Michelle. Often, it wasn't on my agenda to address the situation. Yet, that is exactly what I needed to do as their father, and I would do my best to draw appropriate lines where needed. Sometimes I hit the mark; sometimes, I didn't. I know there were times when I wasn't consistent due to tiredness or simply not knowing what to do. Thankfully, God blessed me with an amazing wife and an incredible mother to our kids who maintained the course. It was her wisdom, encouragement, and willingness that helped to hold me accountable. Our hope in these situations was to lovingly discipline. I believe if you asked them today, they would acknowledge that it was done in love and, although far from perfect, was good for them.

None of the reasons noted above apply to God. God does not doubt Himself, He doesn't tire, He doesn't forget, and we are not a headache to Him. Because God cannot and will not ever change, we know that He will be consistent.

Similar to why consistency from a parent to a child is important, and a blessing to them, God's consistency is a blessing to us. As children of God, we can learn to rely on God. His consistency doesn't just give us a sense of security; it gives us actual tangible security, and it provides us with a clear set of unchanging standards and truths to live by.

As we work through God's attributes and His character traits, we need to remember that He is *all* these attributes *all* the time. Further, God's ability to remain the same integrates into all other aspects of who He is.

Questions:

- What is your current view of God?

- What goes through your mind when dealing with a consistent person? When dealing with a volatile person?

- If God could change, how would this impact your relationship with Him?

2

GOD IS INFINITE AND ETERNAL

"I am the Alpha and the Omega," says the Lord God, "who is, and who was, and who is to come, the Almighty." (Revelation 1:8)

"But do not forget this one thing, dear friends: With the Lord, a day is like a thousand years, and a thousand years are like a day." (2 Peter 3:8)

"For God so loved the world that he gave his one and only Son, that whoever believes in him shall not perish but have eternal life." (John 3:16)

"Do you not know? Have you not heard? The Lord is the everlasting God, the Creator of the ends of the earth. He will not grow tired or weary, and his understanding no one can fathom." (Isaiah 40:28)

"Before the mountains were brought forth, or ever You had formed the earth and the world, even from everlasting to everlasting, You are God." (Psalm 90:2, ESV)

Merriam-Webster defines "infinity" as an unlimited extent of time, space, or quantity.[1] *Boundlessness.*

I recall a conversation I had with one of my uncles when I was a young child. We were driving in his late 1960s blue Camaro. He was an engineer, and he was patiently trying to convey the concept of infinity. I would make up some

---

[1] "Infinity." Merriam-Webster.com Dictionary, Merriam-Webster, https://www.merriam-webster.com/dictionary/infinity, accessed December 8, 2022.

ridiculous number, like 100 billion million quintillion, and he would tell me infinity is greater than that.

I couldn't grasp how there could be no end or limit to something. Yet, that is how it is with God. He is infinite.

Genesis, chapter one, gives us the creation story and tells us how, in the beginning, God created the heavens and the earth and everything in it. This is when time, space and matter came into being. Time commenced "In the beginning". Space was created when God created the heavens, and matter was created when God created the earth. Norm Geisler and Frank Turek in *I Don't Have Enough Faith to Be an Atheist* write, "… since the First Cause created time, space and matter, the First Cause must be outside of time, space and matter. In other words, He is without limits or infinite."[2] Logically this makes sense. To create something, the creator is outside and greater than what he or she creates.

One way to get a glimpse of God's infinite nature is to look at the universe. Genesis 1:16-17 tells us that God created the stars and put them in the expanse of the sky. Scientists estimate that the observable universe is 92 billion light years in diameter.[3] Furthermore, they believe the universe continues to expand and could be as big as 7 trillion light years in diameter. Doing the math, 7 trillion light years is approximately 41,160,000,000,000,000,000,000,000 miles. That's one incredibly large number, one enormous expanding universe, and strong evidence of God's infinite nature. As noted by Geisler and Turek, the First Cause (God) had to be outside time, space and matter to create time space and matter. The sheer size of the universe gives us evidence of God's infinitude.

I thought it would be interesting to consider the opposite spectrum. How small can God make something? Is He able to make something infinitesimally

---

[2] Norm Geisler and Frank Turek, *I Don't Have Enough Faith to Be an Atheist* (Crossway: 2004).
[3] "How Big is the Universe?" Space.com, accessed December 8, 2022, https://www.space.com/24073-how-big-is-the-universe.html.

small? The smallest real thing known to man is the neutrino. A neutrino is a subatomic particle with no electric charge and almost no mass. And then you have a photon that has zero resting mass and moves at the speed of light (and therefore, one might say, is not a thing).[4] The smallest theoretical thing is a Planck particle named after physicist Max Planck. A Planck particle is a hypothetical particle that is extremely small, 10 to the -20th times a proton's radius, and extremely heavy with a mass of 10 to the 19th times a proton's mass.[5] Given that science is considering things that are theoretical or that don't have any mass suggests there are smaller and smaller things created by God that are yet to be identified.

Big or small, God is infinite.

If God were not infinite, He would not be God, just as if He could change, He would not be God. If there were limits to God, that would tell us that there is something greater than God. Hence, He would not be God. Isaiah 40:26 tells us that God won't grow tired or weary. How can that be? Because there is absolutely no limit to Him, His power, His energy, His resources, His love, or His time.

God's infinite nature goes hand in hand with God being eternal. God is immortal. There is nothing that brought God into existence. We see this in Psalm 90:2, "Before the mountains were born or you brought forth the earth and the world, from everlasting to everlasting, You are God." Revelation 1:8 tells us, "'I am the Alpha and the Omega,' says the Lord God, 'who is, and who was, and who is to come, the Almighty.'" There is not a time where He did not exist.

This is a concept with which many people have struggled, including my son. I can remember multiple conversations, when he was young, where he would

---

[4] "What is the smallest existing thing in theory and law?" Physics.Stackexchange, accessed December 8, 2022, https://physics.stackexchange.com/questions/64126/what-is-the-smallest-existing-thing-in-theory-and-law.

[5] "Steady-state model," Wikiland.com, accessed December 8, 2022, https://www.wikiwand.com/en/Planck_particle.

ask who created God. My response would be, "No one," to which he would reply, "How can that be? Someone had to create God." His question made perfect sense as everything else in this world was created and had a beginning except God who is outside time, space, and matter.

Further, there is nothing that can cause God to cease to exist. 1 Timothy 6:15-16 notes that "God, the blessed and only Ruler, the King of kings and Lord of lords, who alone is immortal, and who lives in unapproachable light, whom no one has seen or can see. To Him be honor and glory forever." Here the Bible tells us that God is immortal. God's immortality is consistent with His infinite and eternal nature.

We started the book with a description of God being the Great I AM. Remember Jesus' response to the Jews? "I tell you the truth," Jesus answered, "before Abraham was born, I am!"[6] Knowing that God is everlasting and eternal makes perfect sense and fits with His infinitude. He is, always has been, and always will be. You may be wondering why Jesus is being equated to God. God is comprised of the Trinity, God the Father, God the Son, and God the Holy Spirit. We'll discuss the Trinity in more detail in Chapter Nine.

We see an example of God as infinite and eternal in one of the most quoted verses in the Bible, John 3:16, "For God so loved the world that he gave His only begotten Son so that whosoever believes in Him should not perish but have everlasting life." God's infinite and eternal nature is consistent with this verse and His promise of an eternity in Heaven with Him. It fully aligns with God's promise of an everlasting life with Him in Heaven. If God were not infinite and eternal, then an everlasting life for us in Heaven would be impossible.

Earlier, I mentioned that I believe the Bible is the inerrant Word of God. 1 Timothy 3:16-17 tells us, "All Scripture is God-breathed and is useful for teaching, rebuking, correcting and training in righteousness, so that the servant of God may be thoroughly equipped for every good work." While we are on

---

[6] John 8:58, NLT.

this earth, we are given the opportunity to study God's Word and learn His eternal truths and wisdom. As we study, we know that His words and truth are eternal and will never change.

Even as I write this, I'm feeling convicted. I spend too much time watching sports and reading news feeds on my phone, paying attention to events that are temporary, and not enough time reading and learning God's eternal word and applying His truth to my life. From an eternal investment perspective, why would I not spend more time in His Word?

God's infinitude and eternalness integrate with all aspects of who He is in the same way that He can't change. For instance, God's holiness/goodness (which will be addressed later) is infinite and will never change. What an incredible realization to know that God will always be pure and holy.

Questions:

- What does it mean to have an eternal perspective?
- If you knew you were going to live for an eternity in Heaven with God, would you change your thoughts and actions? Why?
- If so, what would you change?

Mark Chao

3

GOD IS LOVE

"For God so loved the world that he sent his one and only son, that whosoever believes in him may have eternal life." (John 3:16, ESV)

"God is love. Whoever lives in love lives in God and God in them." (1 John 4:16)

"There is no fear in love. But perfect love casts out fear." (1 John 4:18, ESV)

> **<u>Jesus loves me this I know</u>**
> *Jesus loves me this I know*
> *For the Bible tells me so*
> *Little ones to Him belong*
> *They are weak but He is strong*
> *Yes, Jesus loves me*
> *Yes, Jesus loves me*
> *Yes, Jesus loves me*
> *The Bible tells me so.[1]*

I can remember learning this simple song as a young child. As an adult, I think about what an amazing truth this is and the amazing things that come from this truth. God's love is evident throughout the Bible. Nowhere is this love more evident than God sending Jesus to live here on earth and Jesus sacrificing Himself on the cross for each of us.

---

[1] "Jesus Loves Me, This I Know," *Hymnary.org*, accessed July 8, 2021, https://hymnary.org/hymn/BGSS1862/page/67.

As parents, we sacrificially love our children. There's not much we wouldn't do to protect them, and, in fact, some parents go overboard in protecting them. We want the best for our children, even if it means we personally forgo something we want or need in order to ensure they get whatever it is they need or desire. I recently witnessed a father's simple expression of love for his son while on vacation just before Thanksgiving. Early one morning, I was at a restaurant in the hotel getting coffee and tea. I was seated next to this father and his young son, who were enjoying a hot chocolate and a coffee together. His dad asked him a few times whether he was enjoying the hot chocolate. When they got up to leave, the dad stood in front of his son and ran his fingers through his son's hair. It was such a simple act, but it was a physical demonstration of how much this father loved his son.

I think sometimes we only look for God's love in the big things. How often do we miss His kind, loving acts and gifts in the small things? God, our Father in Heaven, wants nothing but the best for us because He loves us, and He demonstrates His love for us in the big things and the little things. We just need to slow down to see evidence of His love.

I started to understand the depth of His love in high school. I went to a Campus Life retreat up in the mountains. The speaker was a man named Jim Zorn. At the time, he was the starting quarterback for the Seattle Seahawks and the father of young children. His message focused on John 3:16. He tried to imagine sacrificing one of his children for someone else. In complete honesty, Jim said there was no way he would sacrifice his child and that he was more likely to sacrifice himself. He then equated this to God sacrificing His Son on the cross to pay for our sins. Worse yet, God knew and saw every bit of what Jesus went through. God loved us so much that he sent His Son to die an incredibly horrific death for us.

Why was Jesus crucified on the cross? In the Old Testament days, the Israelites would sacrifice an animal, often a sheep, goat, or bull, as a burnt offering, sin offering, or guilt offering as commanded by God's law. In many cases, sacrificed animals could not have any defects. The blood of these animals would be ceremonially applied or poured out at the altar for the atonement of sins. Biblical animal sacrifice dealt in whole or in part with the atonement (reparation for a wrong) for the sins of God's chosen people. Jesus, who was and is sinless and without defect, paid the ultimate sacrifice with His blood for the atonement of our sins, past, present, and future. Because of His blood, our sins are forgiven *forever*.

What strikes me is that Jesus voluntarily went to the cross as our sin offering because of His amazing love for you and me. Can you imagine watching a loved one suffer something that was in your control to prevent? That is what God the Father did for us. Romans 5:8 tells us, "But God demonstrates his own love for us in this: While we were still sinners, Christ died for us." God's expression of love for us went way beyond words and way beyond what any of us would or could do. He sent His one and only Son to a brutal death for you and me because He loves us.

According to Psalm 139:1-4, God knows everything about us:

> *O Lord, you have searched me and you know me. You know when I sit and when I rise; you perceive my thoughts from afar. You discern my going out and my lying down. You are familiar with all my ways. Before a word is on my tongue you know it completely, O Lord.*

He knows all the good and the bad, and He loves us no matter what. Pause for a second and hear God's voice telling you He loves you. There is absolutely no doubt that God loves you just the way you are.

How deep is His love? So deep that He sent His Son to the cross as a sacrifice for you and me so that we can spend an eternity in heaven with Him. He also loves us enough to let us decide whether we want to accept this gift. God is a protective father, but not a helicopter parent. He ultimately leaves the decision and consequences up to each of us.

For those of you that are parents, imagine the pain you would feel if your child made a poor decision and had to suffer the consequences. Why do you feel that pain? Because you love your child.

I can't imagine how much it pains God each time one of His children decides not to follow Him and suffers the consequences. Why? Because of His unimaginable love for each one of us. God's love for us is also expressed through His compassion. He feels what we feel. A good example of this comes from the shortest verse in the Bible, John 11:35, "Jesus wept."

Prior to this verse, John writes that Jesus had been told His good friend Lazarus was ill. Mary and Martha, Lazarus' sisters, sent word to Jesus in the hope that Jesus would come and heal him. Jesus had a plan. He knew Lazarus was going to die and that He would raise Lazarus back to life to glorify God. Jesus stayed where He was for a few more days, and by the time He finally arrived, Lazarus had been in the tomb for four days. Mary and others came to Jesus weeping and in deep grief. At this moment, Jesus wept too. If Jesus knew He was going to raise Lazarus from the dead, why did He weep? I think there are two reasons.

First, He wept because He loved Mary and the others. He felt the pain and grief they felt and shared in it. In the same way, Jesus loves us and shares our grief and our joy. Second, I believe Jesus wept to set an example to us that we should weep with those who are weeping and share the joy with those who are celebrating (Romans 12:15).

Our children will sometimes run to us when they are scared or when they have had a nightmare. I can remember, on a number of nights, being woken up by a frightened child that had just had a scary dream. They were frightened and wanted the loving comfort of mom or dad. Sometimes we would pull them up into bed with us; other times, we would walk them back to their bed and sit with them for a bit until they calmed down and went back to sleep. Often, in a cloud of sleepiness, we would pray with them.

As adults, where do we turn when we are afraid? We turn to God. As I'm drafting this, we are recovering from the COVID-19 pandemic with a global instability that we haven't seen since the Cold War. I'm confident there are a number of prayers being said in these uncertain times. This is a great time to remember 1 John 4:18. "There is no fear in love. But perfect love casts out fear." The only perfect love I know of is God's love. When we turn to God and experience His comforting love, we have nothing to fear. Sometimes we experience that love directly from God. Other times, God's love flows through someone in our lives. Regardless, His love is a love that will last for an eternity. While we are on this earth and potentially fearing pandemics, violence, war, illness, divorce, job insecurity or whatever it is, know that God's love is above all.

What's amazing is that you have access to God's never-ending love if you have accepted Jesus as your Savior. Romans 5:5 says, "and hope does not put us to shame, because God's love has been poured into our hearts through the Holy Spirit who has been given to us."[2] Have you ever noticed that when you perform an act of service sheerly out of obligation, you tire and maybe even feel resentment? But that same act of service, if performed in God's love, leaves you feeling energized? Why? Because you're being filled with God's never-ending love.

One of my longstanding prayers is that our children would know and feel God's incredible love for them. When they were kids, I would often ask them a question after I did something for or with them. The question I asked was, "Why did I do this for you?" They would respond, "Because you love me." I would then ask them this question, "Who loves you more?" Their answer? "God." I hope they will always know how much this imperfect father loves them and, more importantly, that the perfect Father loves them in ways they can't even imagine and more than anyone they will ever know. I pray that you, too, would know how much your perfect Father in Heaven loves you.

From the previous chapters, we know that God never changes and that He is infinite. Now, let's combine these two attributes with God's love. Imagine, God's love is infinite. There is no limit to His love for us, and His love for us will never, ever end. Let's add to that the fact that God is unchanging. That

---

[2] ESV.

tells us His limitless love for us will never change. He will love you and me, no matter what. There is nothing we can do to lose His love.

Questions

- Have you ever experienced unconditional love? Conditional love? What happened, and what was the impact on you?
- Do you believe you can earn God's love?
- Do you love God? Unconditionally?

4

GOD IS ALL-POWERFUL (OMNIPOTENT)

"Listen to me, O Jacob, Israel, whom I have called; I am he; I am the first and the last. My own hand laid the foundation of the earth, and my right hand spread out the heavens; when I summon them, they all stand up together." (Isaiah 48:12-13)

When you think of power, what do you think of? It could be the most powerful person on the planet, arguably a leader from the United States, China, or Russia. It could be a weapon such as an atomic bomb. How about the strongest animal on the earth? A blue whale? Do you perhaps think of natural disasters like tornadoes, hurricanes, or earthquakes. What about the sun? According to NASA's Cosmicopia, the sun generates 5 x 10 to the 23rd horsepower per second. This is enough power to melt a bridge of ice two miles wide and one-mile-thick extending from the sun to the moon in one second.[1] Speaking of horsepower, what about a car? Several production cars have recently exceeded the 300 miles per hour mark, including the Bugatti Chiron and a Koenigsegg 125 Jesko. Each of these cars has a 1600-horsepower engine. Probably even more impressive was that a 2006 Ford GT retrofitted with 2500 horsepower hit the 300 mph mark a couple of months before these other cars. All of this is child's play compared to God's power.

The single most powerful item noted above is the sun. It is estimated that there are 1 x 10^{24} stars in the universe.[2] That's a one followed by 24 zeros.

---

[1]   "Sun," Cosmicopia.gsfc.nasa.gov, accessed December 14, 2022, https://cosmicopia.gsfc.nasa.gov/qa_sun.html#power.

[2]   "How Many Stars Are There?" Space.com, accessed December 14, 2022, https://www.space.com/26078-how-many-stars-are-there.html.

Remember, we think of the sun as incredibly powerful, yet our sun is just one of an outrageous number of powerful stars. Genesis 1 tells us God created the heavens and the earth including the stars. God created each and every one of these incredibly powerful stars. His power created these stars, and yet we have a hard time comprehending the power of a *single* star, our sun.

Here's where it gets fun. When we combine God's infinitude with His power, we can only conclude that God's power is limitless and never-ending. Now, when we think of God creating the heavens and the earth, it doesn't seem far-fetched at all. Rather, it makes perfect sense.

The Bible reflects God's power in Psalm 147:5: "Great is our Lord and mighty in power; His understanding has no limit." Just as His understanding has no limit, His power also has no limit. It is comforting to know God has no equal, especially when we think about end times.

Revelation 3:7 tells us, "What he opens no one can shut, and what he shuts no one can open." Said another way, nothing and no one can get in God's way and stop Him from exercising His will. In fact, God uses His power to perform miracles like feeding the 5000, turning water into wine, curing lepers, and restoring sight.[3] The most powerful miracle of all time is the resurrection of Jesus.

Ephesians 1:19-20 states, "That power is the same as the mighty strength He exerted when He raised Christ from the dead and seated Him at His right hand in the heavenly realms…" God's power is unstoppable, and, in the end, we know He wins!

God's power can be witnessed via miracles. I have been blessed to be connected to a Christian ministry for a number of years called Children's Hunger Fund (CHF). CHF was founded by Dave Phillips in 1992. Shortly after its founding, Dave received a phone call from the director of a cancer treatment center in Honduras asking for a specific cancer drug. The director

---

[3] Matthew 14:13-21; John 2:1-11; Luke 17:11-19; John 9.

explained that there were seven children that needed this drug and that they would die without it. Dave told the director that he did not know how he could obtain this drug. They ended the phone call with a prayer. Literally, as soon as he hung up the phone, it rang again. It was a pharmaceutical company based in New Jersey asking Dave if he would have any use for 48,000 vials of a cancer drug. Not just any cancer drug, *but the exact same drug that Dave and the director had just prayed about.*[4] A coincidence? No. It was a miracle with God's fingerprints all over it.

As I was researching miracles, I came across a story that involved Ruth Graham (the daughter of Billy Graham). Ruth Graham wrote she was at a church picnic, and the pastor's wife discovered that the diamond from her wedding ring was missing. Those present gathered in prayer and then proceeded to search the picnic site to no avail. The group came back the next day to search again with the same result. The diamond was gone. The following week, after it had rained and the grass had been mowed, Ruth Graham's daughter was playing in the same area. She spotted a shiny object in the grass and thought it was a rhinestone from her doll's outfit. She brought it inside to her mom, and you guessed it, it was the lost diamond.[5] (Whether this story qualifies as a miracle, I'm not sure, but it does show that God intervenes in people's lives.)

Interestingly, I have a similar story to Ruth's involving my wedding band. One Saturday morning, I played golf. At the end of the round, I searched my pockets for my wedding band and discovered I had lost it somewhere on the golf course. Sharing this with Michelle, who was pregnant with our oldest, was not one of my better marriage-building moments.

Several months went by, and Michelle and I agreed that it was time to replace the ring. Right after this conversation, I called the pro shop at the golf course to schedule a tee time. The assistant pro, Mike, answered my call and asked

---

[4] Francis Chan, *Forgotten God* (David C. Cook: 2009), 135–136.

[5] "12 Absolutely Amazing Miracles," Beliefnet.com, accessed December 28, 2022, https://www.beliefnet.com/faiths/galleries/12-absolutely-amazing-miracles.aspx.

me to describe my wedding band. Mike happened to be the only person at the course that I had told about my lost ring at the time it happened. The ring I described was the ring Mike found. He was giving a lesson and took a practice swing on the tee box. He took a divot and, lo and behold, dug up my ring with his practice swing. God's fingerprints strike again!

You may be thinking, and rightfully so, that this was pure coincidence and luck. And you may well be right, but I don't believe in coincidences knowing that God is all-powerful. This golf course is 6,500 yards in distance and covers 150 acres. If you knew my golf game, I likely covered all 150 acres that day. Mike's practice swing was at the exact spot where my wedding ring had been buried for several months. That day, God had a unique way of reminding me of his power. This was a miracle, pure and simple. I learned a few things, too: First, I no longer take off my wedding band when I play golf, and second, every time I look at my ring, I'm reminded that God wanted me to have it back and how blessed I am by Him through my marriage to Michelle.

Now here's the crazy part: God's power, like His love, is available to you and me. The Bible makes this point more than once. For instance, God provides us with His strength and power so we can accomplish His will. It may be that accomplishing God's will means dealing with a difficult situation by relying on God's strength. Paul, in his letter to the Philippians, wrote, "I can do everything through Him who strengthens me."[6] Realize that Paul wrote Philippians while he was in a Roman prison. There should be no doubt that he was relying on God's strength to get him through that time. In today's world, this difficulty could be an illness, divorce, joblessness, or betrayal. Remember, we can get through these times because God strengthens us. Not only that, God's provision of His power is available to us on an ongoing basis. The book of Isaiah summarizes this well, "But those who hope in the Lord will renew their strength. They will soar like eagles, they will run and not grow weary,

---

[6] Philippians 4:13, ESV.

they will walk and not be faint."[7] If we put our hope in God, he promises us to renew our strength and that we will not tire.

With God's strength and power at work in us, He is able to accomplish things through us we can't even dream of. Ephesians 3:20 notes that "Glory belongs to God whose power is at work in us. By this power He can do infinitely more than we can ask or imagine."[8] God's power is so far beyond us, we can't get close to imagining the things He can do. I don't know about you, but this seems like a challenge to us as believers. Let's expand our dreams and see what God can accomplish through us. As Pastor Rick Warren is fond of saying, "No dream is too big for God."

Growing up, there used to be a playground argument over whose dad was the strongest. Well, that argument is settled once and for all. I AM is the strongest dad there is.

Questions:

- What's the most powerful thing or moment you have experienced?

- Have you ever experienced a miracle or intervention from God? What happened?

- Knowing God's power is available to you, what is your dream?

---

[7] Isaiah 40:31.
[8] GWT.

Mark Chao

5

GOD IS ALL-KNOWING
(OMNISCIENT)

If I asked you to name the smartest person that ever lived, you would likely say Albert Einstein. Just for fun, I decided to do an internet search and entered the phrase "smartest person who ever lived." I came across a website, Bigthink.com, that published a list of the top 20 plus smartest people of all time. This site estimates that this list of individuals had IQs of 190 and above. Some of the individuals noted on this list include Leonardo da Vinci, the first Renaissance man, Sir Isaac Newton, Plato, Aristotle, Marie Curie, and Galileo. These individuals' contributions to math, science, physics, art, astronomy, and philosophy are well known. However, a couple of the individuals included on the list surprised me, such as Cleopatra, Shakespeare, and Confucius.

Interestingly, one of the individuals noted on this list was Gottfried Leibniz. He lived from 1646 to 1716 and was a philosopher and mathematician best known for inventing calculus. As a philosopher, he wrote on theodicy (the justification of God's goodness and power in light of the existence of evil). He concluded that we lived in the best possible universe that God could have created.[1] Leibniz believed that because God is all-knowing, "He does nothing without acting in accordance with supreme reasoning." In other words, because God is all knowing, He knew the outcome of every possible scenario and then created the best world possible.

One person that gets overlooked routinely as being one of the smartest people who ever lived is Jesus. In fact, He is the smartest person to ever walk this

---

[1] Paul Ratner, "Top 20 Smartest People Who Ever Lived," BigThink.com, accessed December 19, 2022, https://bigthink.com/paul-ratner/top-20-smartest-people-who-ever-lived.

earth. Dallas Willard does a fantastic job of addressing this in *The Divine Conspiracy* writing:

> *The biblical and continuing vision of Jesus was of one who made all of created reality and kept it working, literally "holding it together" (Col 1:17). And today we think people are smart who make light bulbs and computer chips and rockets out of "stuff" already provided! He made "the stuff"!*

> *...At the literally mundane level, Jesus knew how to transform the molecular structure of water to make it wine. That knowledge also allowed him to take a few pieces of bread and some little fish and feed thousands of people. He could create matter from the energy he knew how to access from "the heavens," right where he was.*

> *He is not just nice, he is brilliant. He is the smartest man who ever lived. He is now supervising the entire course of world history (Rev. 1:5) while simultaneously preparing the rest of the universe for our future role in it (John 14:2). He always has the best information on everything and certainly also on the things that matter most in human life.[2]*

Willard acknowledges that Jesus is nice. This is the Jesus most people think of, a loving and caring Jesus. But Willard challenges us to rethink this picture. Not only is Jesus nice, but He is the smartest, most intelligent human being to ever live. He knows EVERYTHING. With this knowledge, He created all that we see or the "stuff" that goes into everything we see. He used this knowledge to perform miracles, including turning water into wine and feeding thousands with a couple of fish and loaves.

I think Isaiah 40:13-14 does an incredible job of describing God's omniscience: "Who has understood the mind of the Lord, instructed him as his counselor? Whom did the Lord consult to enlighten him, and who taught him the right way? Who was it that taught him knowledge or showed him the path of understanding?" The obvious answer is no one. Remember that God created

---

[2] Dallas Willard, *The Divine Conspiracy* (San Francisco: Harper, 1998), 94–95.

the universe and everything in it by speaking it into being.[3] He is the ultimate source of knowledge and understanding.

God designed the many complexities that we see in the world around us. All those incredible scientific discoveries that we continue to make are as simple as adding one plus one to God. As much as man tries, and as much as man's ego doesn't want to admit it, we cannot and will not ever come anywhere close to God's knowledge. Simply put, God knows everything from the most minute detail to the largest, most complex formula or concept.

The knowledge that was required to create the universe and all that is in it is beyond anything that we can comprehend. I was speaking with my son, who was a medical student at the time. We got on the subject of the human cell, and he said that the more he learned about the human cell and how it functions, the more he realized how little he knew. If we just consider the complex human brain and simple amoeba, the intricacies and knowledge necessary to design them are remarkable. An article by NewScientist addresses the complexities of the brain:

> *The brain is the most complex organ in the human body. It produces our every thought, action, memory, feeling and experience of the world. This jelly-like mass of tissue, weighing in at around 1.4 kilograms, contains a staggering one hundred billion nerve cells, or neurons.*

> *The complexity of the connectivity between these cells is mind-boggling. Each neuron can make contact with thousands or even tens of thousands of others, via tiny structures called synapses. Our brains form a million new connections for every second of our lives. The pattern and strength of the connections is constantly changing and no two brains are alike...[4]*

Helen Philips's article, "Introduction: The Human Brain," describes one of the most fascinating competitions pitting the human brain against

---

[3] Genesis 1.

[4] Helen Philips, "Introduction: The Human Brain," New Scientist.com, accessed December 12, 2022, https://www.newscientist.com/article/dn9969-introduction-the-human-brain/.

supercomputers. At the time the article was published, the fastest supercomputer was the Tianhe-2. It could process information at a speed of 54.902 petaFlops. According to the article, a petaFlop can process a "quadrillion (one thousand trillion) floating point calculations per second."[5] Even at that unbelievable speed, the human brain is incalculably faster. The article states that the human brain can potentially make the equivalent of a billion billion calculations every second! To put this in perspective, in 2014, an experiment in Japan revealed that the world's fourth fastest supercomputer took 40 minutes to calculate what takes the human brain a single second to calculate.[6]

What a wonderful and complex creation our brains are! Right now, your brain is allowing you to read and process these words! All because we have an amazing God that knows everything and that designed our brains.

You may be thinking, "Well, what about artificial intelligence?" That is a great question. So much is being done with AI at a speed that is arguably quicker than a human brain and with access to more data. Yet, AI will never be able to outthink or outperform God because AI will never have more knowledge than God. The data that AI accesses comes from humans, and unlike God, humans are limited in their knowledge. The other thought that is worthy of note is that we, as believers in Jesus as our Savior, have access to God's mind. 1 Corinthians 2:16 tells us: "For who has known the mind of the Lord that he may instruct him?' But we have the mind of Christ."[7] Through Christ, God is able to provide us His wisdom and knowledge when He so desires. As we come to know God, we can trust that He will give us access to His thoughts at the right time.

---

[5] Ibid.

[6] John Staughton, "The Human Brain vs. Supercomputers... Which One Wins?" Science ABC.com, accessed December 12, 2022, https://www.scienceabc.com/humans/the-human-brain-vs-supercomputers-which-one-wins.html.

[7] Credit for this thought goes to Matt Kyser, my pastor at Village Church of Irvine, based on a discussion we were having on AI.

Let's now go from the incredibly complex human brain to a simple single-cell amoeba often referred to as the lowest form of life. The amount of information contained in a single-cell amoeba is mind-boggling. Norman Geisler and Frank Turek in *I Don't Have Enough Faith to Be an Atheist* write:

> *The incredible specified complexity of life becomes obvious when one considers the message found in the DNA of a one-celled amoeba (a creature so small, several hundred could be lined up in an inch). Staunch Darwinist Richard Dawkins, professor of zoology at Oxford University, admits that the message found in just the cell nucleus of a tiny amoeba is more than all thirty volumes of the Encyclopedia Britannica combined, and the entire amoeba has as much information in its DNA as 1,000 complete sets of the Encyclopedia Britannica![8]*

Interestingly, Bill Gates made the following statement regarding DNA: "DNA is like a computer program, but far, far more advanced than any software we've ever created."[9]

When we consider the highest and lowest forms of life, and the complexities, processes, and knowledge that the Creator possesses to design them, we are left in awe. Yet more important than this is that we also need to personalize God's knowledge. Through God's knowledge and power, He created you and me. Ephesians 2:10 says, in part, "For we are God's masterpiece..."[10] In Psalm 139:14, David writes, "I praise you because I am fearfully and wonderfully made; your works are wonderful." These verses apply equally to all of us. We are all fearfully and wonderfully made by God.

Not only does God know us physically, but he also knows each and every detail of our lives. Psalm 139:1-4 says "O Lord, you have searched me and

---

[8] Norman L. Geisler, "Quotes," *I Don't Have Enough Faith to Be an Atheist*, GoodReads.com, accessed December 12, 2022, https://www.goodreads.com/quotes/8169535-the-incredible-specified-complexity-of-life-becomes-obvious-when-one.

[9] Bill Gates, "The Road Ahead Quotes," Goodreads.com, accessed December 12, 2022, https://www.goodreads.com/work/quotes/1479853-the-road-ahead.

[10] NLT.

you know me. You know when I sit and when I rise, you perceive my thoughts from afar. You discern my going out and my lying down; you are familiar with all my ways. Before a word is on my tongue you know it completely, O Lord." [11] He knows the number of hairs on our head, including my ever-decreasing number. He knows what we're going to say before we say it. He knows our thoughts and our deepest concerns. He knows every secret about us. He knows our hearts and our intentions. He knows every wrong we've ever done and every sin we've ever committed. However, He still loves us beyond anything we can imagine, and there is nothing we can do to lose that love.

Another facet of knowledge is wisdom. "Wisdom" is defined as the soundness of an action or decision with regard to the application of experience, knowledge, and good judgment.[12] Proverbs 2:6 tells us, "For the Lord gives wisdom and from His mouth come knowledge and understanding." The wisest man ever to live is King Solomon. In 1 Kings, we learn that there was never anyone like Solomon, nor will there ever be another like him.[13] (God told Solomon to ask for whatever he would like. Solomon asked for a discerning heart to govern his people and to distinguish right from wrong. The Lord was pleased with this response because Solomon did not ask for riches. As a result, God gave Solomon a discerning heart and wisdom unlike anyone before or after him and also blessed him with incredible riches.) Similar to God being greater than and outside anything He has created, God cannot give away more wisdom than he possesses. So, it stands to reason that God is not only all-knowing, but that God is also the wisest. God cannot gain any more wisdom because His wisdom is infinite and He is unchanging and perfect. God is able to apply His knowledge, which results in wisdom beyond anything our limited minds can understand.

As parents, we use our limited wisdom to guide and protect our children. Similar to Solomon, whatever wisdom we possess comes from God. How

---

[11] Luke 12:7.
[12] "Wisdom," Oxford Learners Dictionaries.com, accessed December 12, 2022, https://www.oxfordlearnersdictionaries.com/us/definition/american_english/wisdom.
[13] 1 King 3:12.

fortunate, then, that we have a loving God who possesses unlimited wisdom, a God that wants to guide and protect us and does so out of truly knowing what is best for us. In Psalm 32:8, God tells us, "I will guide you along the best path for your life. I will watch over you and advise you." God has shared this wisdom through His Word. When we are confused, hopeless, or don't know what to do, we have the opportunity to turn to our Heavenly Father, who is all-knowing. When we have questions about how best to live a godly life, answers are available to us in the Bible. We would be wise to study His Word and apply His wisdom to our lives.

Questions:

- Who knows you the best? Do they know everything about you?

- What are the implications to you of God's wisdom and knowledge?

- Are you comforted or frightened by the fact that God knows everything about you?

Mark Chao

6

GOD IS EVERYWHERE (OMNIPRESENT)

" 'Who can hide in secret places so that I cannot see him?' declares the Lord. 'Do not I fill heaven and earth?' declares the Lord." (Jeremiah 23:24)

"...because God has said, 'Never will I leave you; never will I forsake you.'" (Hebrews 13:5)

"So do not fear, for I am with you; do not be dismayed, for I am your God, I will strengthen you and help you; I will uphold you with my righteous right hand." (Isaiah 41:10)

"Where can I go from your Spirit? Where can I flee from your presence? If I go up to the heavens, you are there; if I make my bed in the depths, you are there. If I rise on the wings of dawn, if I settle on the far side of the sea, even there your hand will guide me, your right hand will hold me fast." (Psalm 139:7-10)

At this point, we know that God is never changing, love, infinite/eternal, all powerful, and knows everything. He is also everywhere. Knowing God is everywhere makes sense in that He created everything and is beyond everything. At this point, it's worth repeating Geisler and Turke's words quoted in Chapter 2, "... since the First Cause (in this case God) created time, space and matter, the First Cause must be outside of time, space and matter. In other words, He is without limits or infinite."[1] God's omnipresence is consistent with His infinitude. Since God is outside of space, time, and matter,

---

[1] Norm Geisler and Frank Turek, *I Don't Have Enough Faith to Be an Atheist* (Crossway: 2004).

He is literally beyond the universe. God is able to watch over everything because He is here, there, and everywhere. This is evidenced in Jeremiah 23:24 referenced at the beginning of the chapter.

Just as God's presence in our lives is important, the importance of a parent's presence in a child's life also cannot be overemphasized. The benefits to a child of a loving, present, and attentive parent include a strong sense of security and comfort when they are scared, and direction as they grow. An unfortunate development in the world of parenting is helicopter parents. They seem like they are ever-present and always hovering around their children, waiting to swoop in to fix a problem, correct a perceived wrong, get their child more playing time on a team, or make sure their child receives some type of advantage. In these situations, it's usually more about the parent than the child. Often, the parent is living their life through their child. In fact, helicopter parents have even started showing up in their adult child's workplaces. I've spoken to human resource managers at the company I work for, and they've told me that parents have accompanied their children to interviews and that some have tried to intervene on behalf of their children during performance evaluation periods. From my perspective, this type of parenting stunts the growth of a child as they don't get the opportunity to problem solve and handle difficulties on their own.

Like a helicopter parent, God is present, but unlike many helicopter parents, He exercises ultimate wisdom. As we read in the prior chapter, there is no one wiser than God. Add to this the comfort knowing that God is always with each of us. He is walking with us each step of the way. God is the perfect loving, present, and attentive parent, "God is our refuge and strength, an ever-present help in trouble. Therefore we will not fear, though the earth give way and the mountains fall into the heart of the sea."[2]

There are several promises in the Bible that are only possible if God is with us. Jesus tells us, "Come to me, all you who are weary and burdened, and I

---

[2] Psalm 46:1-2.

will give you rest. Take my yoke upon you and learn from me, for I am gentle and humble in heart, and you will find rest for your souls. For my yoke is easy and my burden is light."[3] How is it that we can be yoked to Jesus? It's because He is omnipresent and always with us. If we yoke ourselves to Jesus, we will learn from Him how to be gentle and humble in heart. Not only that, but the burdens of this world will become lighter when we walk side by side with Jesus. Jesus wants us to share our burdens with Him, and we can do this because He is with us.

He even promises to uphold us with His righteous right hand when we are weak or afraid, "So do not fear, for I am with you; do not be dismayed, for I am your God, I will strengthen you and help you; I will uphold you with my righteous right hand."[4] We can only be upheld by someone that is constantly at our side.

God also promises to guide us with His right hand, to hold us fast. The psalmist David wrote "Where can I go from your Spirit? Where can I flee from your presence? If I go up to the heavens, you are there; if I make my bed in the depths, you are there. If I rise on the wings of dawn, if I settle on the far side of the sea, even there your hand will guide me, your right hand will hold me fast."[5] No matter where we go, even beyond the far side of the seas, God is there.

When we need direction, God is there. When we need assurance and comfort, God is there. How can we be sure of this? Because God promises multiple times that He will not leave us alone. Four times, God declares that He is with us and will never leave us or forsake us.

---

[3] Matthew 11:28.
[4] Isaiah 41:10.
[5] Psalm 139:7-10.

"Be strong and courageous. Do not be afraid or terrified because of them, for the Lord your God goes with you; he will never leave you nor forsake you." (Deuteronomy 31:6)

"The Lord himself goes before you and will be with you; he will never leave you nor forsake you. Do not be afraid; do not be discouraged." (Deuteronomy 31:8)

"As I was with Moses, so I will be with you; I will never leave you nor forsake you." (Joshua 1:5)

"Never will I leave you; never will I forsake you." (Hebrews 13:5)

For those who need assurance, it doesn't get any better than this. The God of the universe wants to leave no doubt in our minds that *He is always with us and will not abandon us.*

Recently, I was at a Christian concert, and Tauren Wells posed the question, "Why does God speak to us in whispers?" His answer, because He's right next to us.

Along the same lines, I remember hearing a story about Hebrews 13:5 some years ago. A speaker was sharing a story about a time he had shared the Gospel with a man who was not yet a believer. He shared Hebrews 13:5 and told the man to focus on this verse (which he did). The man read the verse over and over throughout the night. By the time the sun rose the next morning, he had accepted Jesus as his Savior. The power of this promise overwhelmed him.

Take some time and repeat this verse in your mind. Focus on the promise and what it means; God will never leave you and never turn His back on you. When you are experiencing joy, know that God shares your joy. When you are afraid, know that God is holding you with His righteous right hand, He will strengthen you, and you do not need to be afraid.[6] When you are uncertain

---

[6] Isaiah 41:10.

about what to do, you can turn to God and seek His guidance.[7] When you are anxious or worried, you can access God's peace that surpasses all understanding.[8] I will always remember God's peace covering me in the midst of my job change as I wrote about in the Foreward.

I'm going to digress here from God's omnipresence and focus on God's promise to never forsake us. One of the last things Jesus said on the cross was a verse from Psalm 22, "My God my god, why have you forsaken me."[9] God will never forsake us, yet he forsook Jesus. I'm so thankful that we will never have to experience this. What makes me even more thankful is the realization that God the Father loves us so much. So much so, that He forsook His own Son.

The words contained in Psalm 23:4, one of the most well-known and beautiful scriptures in the Bible, says, "Even though I walk through the valley of the shadow of death, I will fear no evil, for you are with me, your rod and your staff, they comfort me." These words are not an empty promise or wishful thinking. Psalm 23 is not a letter from a friend saying, "I am with you." No, *God is actually here with you as you read this, and He is here with me as I write this.* He is with us every step of the way, and I would submit that is why this Psalm provides so much comfort.

There is one more verse I would like to share with you about God's presence. Zephaniah 3:17 says, "The Lord your God is in your midst; He is a warrior who can deliver. He takes great delight in you; He renews you by His love; he shouts for joy over you."[10] God is in our midst; He is right here with us. Why? Because He enjoys being with you. I equate it to parents spending time with their children and the joy that a parent feels just watching their child. God delights in being with us. As a warrior, He protects us. Not only that, but He

---

[7] Psalm 139: 7-10.

[8] Philippians 4:6.

[9] Matthew 27:46.

[10] NET.

also comforts and cares for us with His love. And finally, He shouts for joy over us.

Imagine that the God of the universe is shouting for joy over you. He is the ultimate encourager. Just as parents encourage their children, God is absolutely encouraging you and cheering you on.

Sometimes it seems that God isn't with us. We don't feel His presence, we don't hear His voice, we don't see Him at work. Why might this be the case? There could be a number of reasons that are part of His plan and way beyond our comprehension. It could also be that we've been ignoring Him or that we are in sin. My experience and the experiences I have observed in other believers require us to make one or more of the following changes when it feels difficult to hear God:

- Spend regular quiet time with God reading His word and praying.
- Slow down and make room for God in interactions with others.
- Stay connected to other believers who will encourage us and hold us accountable.
- Confess our sins to God, experience His forgiveness, and do our best not to repeat it.

In Matthew 28:20, Jesus promises us, "And surely I am with you always, to the very end of the age." God hasn't left us. Know without a shadow of a doubt that He is right here with us because He is omnipresent.

Questions:

- Have you ever had a close friend/relationship desert you in a time of need? What happened?
- Knowing that God is always with you, how does this make you feel? Do you experience anxiety, fear, a sense of comfort? Why?

7

GOD IS FAITHFUL

"Know therefore that the Lord your God is God, the faithful God who keeps covenant and steadfast love with those who love him and keep his commandments, to a thousand generations." (Deuteronomy 7:9, ESV)

"If we are faithless, he remains faithful—for he cannot deny himself." (2 Timothy 2:13, ESV)

"They are new every morning; great is your faithfulness." (Lamentations 3:23, ESV)

"God is faithful, by whom you were called into the fellowship of his Son, Jesus Christ our Lord." (1 Corinthians 1:9, ESV)

"But you, O Lord, are a God merciful and gracious, slow to anger and abounding in steadfast love and faithfulness." (Psalm 86:15, ESV)

"The Lord is always good. He is always loving and kind, and his faithfulness goes on and on to each succeeding generation." (Psalm 100:5, TLB)

"God is not a man, that he should lie, nor a son of man that he should change his mind. Does he speak and then not act? Does he promise and not fulfill?" (Numbers 23:19, BSB)

"The LORD is trustworthy in all he promises..." (Psalm 145:13)

Merriam-Webster defines the word "faithful" as steadfast in affection or allegiance, firm in adherence to promises, or in observance of duty.[1]

As a dad, I've always tried my best to be faithful and keep any promises I made to my children. This was important to me as I wanted my children to learn they could trust me and my word and that they could count on their dad. Why? Because I wanted them to have a sense of security and confidence in me. I'm far from perfect and didn't keep every promise, but I hope I kept enough of them that they know I will always try to be there for them. I would be devastated if this weren't the case.

My goal as a father was to be there for my children because I knew firsthand what it was like to have a father that did not keep his promises and was not faithful. Please know that I loved my dad, and in his own way, he loved me. He passed away in 1998. I learned generosity from him as well as the fun and adventure of trying different foods. I passed these on to my children. That said, my dad was not faithful to my mom and broke his covenant of marriage on more than one occasion. As a result, my parents divorced when I was ten years old. My dad also broke the promises and commitments he had made to my siblings and me. It got to the point where I expected he would not keep his word to minimize the disappointment. His unfaithfulness left a mark.

This is a huge contrast to our Father in heaven. 2 Timothy 2:13 tells us that "He remains faithful, for he cannot disown himself." Deuteronomy 7:9 says, "Know therefore that the Lord your God is God: He is the faithful God, keeping his covenant of love to a thousand generations of those who love Him and keep His commands." God, our Father, cannot and will not break a promise giving us comfort, a sense of security, and a deep-rooted confidence. We can absolutely trust God because He is faithful.

---

[1] "Faithful," Merriam-Webster.com, accessed December 12, 2022, https://www.merriam-webster.com/dictionary/faithful.

I've heard it mentioned by Rick Warren, founder of Saddleback Church, that there are over 7000 promises in the Bible. We can count on each and every one of these promises.

In the foreword, I wrote of a time when I experienced God's fulfillment of one of His promises. I was going through an incredibly difficult time at work and was ultimately forced to resign from my position. I faced a number of uncertainties, including finding a new job, selling a home, buying a home, and bringing a second child into the world. To make matters more interesting, we were attempting to sell our home when September 11 occurred, and we had already signed a non-contingent offer to purchase a new home.

One morning, in the midst of all this chaos, I was reading through the Bible and came across Philippians 4:6. It says, "Do not be anxious about anything, but in everything by prayer and petition, with thanksgiving, present your requests to God. And the peace of God, which transcends all understanding, will guard your hearts and minds in Christ Jesus." After reading these words, I took a moment to pray and thanked God for who He is. I thanked Him that I could trust in Him and His plan, whatever that may be. Immediately, I felt a peace that made absolutely no sense other than the fulfillment of God's promise to protect my heart and my mind.

I have no doubt that I can trust God and every one of His promises. I've developed this trust for several reasons. First, I've experienced God's fulfillment of His promise of peace as well as other promises. Experiencing God's repeated fulfillment of promises has caused me to deeply trust in Him. Secondly, I know God's character and that He is a reliable Father. When we start to combine God's character and attributes, the only reasonable conclusion we can reach is that He is capable of and will keep each and every promise contained in the Bible.

Up to this point, we have read that God is unchanging, that He is infinite, that He loves us, that He is with us, that He is all-knowing, and that He is all-powerful. So, to think that God is faithful to all His promises fits perfectly with who He is.

Because God is unchanging, He can't suddenly be unfaithful.

Because God knows everything, He knows the impact of His promises and would not make them if they could not be kept. Further, He knows how each promise should be fulfilled because of His knowledge.

Because God is all-powerful, He is able to execute on each and every promise. (Psalm 143:13 reminds us that God is faithful to ALL His promises.) I mentioned earlier that I was not able to keep every promise to my children. Usually, it was because of a circumstance beyond my control. God doesn't encounter this.

Because He is always with us, He knows when we are coming to Him for a promise. I'm a bit hesitant here because I don't want to leave the impression that God is like a genie in a bottle and we can make Him do things. He will ultimately keep His promise, but not necessarily in our desired time frame.

Because He loves us, His promises are promises a loving father would make to his children. Promises that are good for us, help us, that ultimately cause us to trust Him, and draw us closer to Him. Because He is faithful, He will keep His promises. The challenge to us is to get to know these promises so we can call on them. How do we go about this? We need to learn and memorize the promises contained in the Bible. I've listed several promises below to get us started.

John 16:24 states, "Until now you have not asked for anything in my name. Ask and you will receive, and your joy will be complete." God always hears our prayers and answers. I heard someone say that if God does not answer the way we want, He answers with what we would have wanted if we knew everything that He knows.

In the previous chapter, we read through several of God's promises about not leaving us or forsaking us, including Hebrews 13:5, "Never will I leave you, never will I forsake you." What does this mean, and why is it so comforting? It means that God promises to always be with us. He will not leave us. This fits with His omnipresence. Equally important, God promises that He will never reject us. He will not quit on us. He will not disown us. It's incredibly comforting to know that God is right there with us no matter what we're going through or what we've done. We are His.

John 3:16 has to be one of the most quoted verses/promises in the Bible, and it probably gets the most press. It states, "For God so loved the world that he gave His only Son, so that whosoever believes in Him will have everlasting life." Why is it cited time and again? Because it contains God's promise of eternal life. He promises eternal life with Him if we believe that Jesus died for our sins and that He is our Lord and Savior.

John 14:2 says, "In my Father's house are many rooms; if it were not so, I would have told you. I am going there to prepare a place for you." This is a promise that we will not experience on this side of Heaven.[2] I have included it because I am hoping that it will give you a glimpse of Heaven.[3] We have all seen an incredible sunrise/sunset or a beautiful landscape surrounding us. These will pale in comparison to what we will see and experience when we get to Heaven and the place prepared for us.

Now consider Philippians 4:6-7: "Do not be anxious about anything, but in everything, by prayer and petition, with thanksgiving, present your requests to God. And the peace of God, which transcends all understanding, will guard your hearts and your minds in Christ Jesus." I've included this Scripture here again because there are two things I wanted to point out. The first is that God wants us to bring *everything* to Him. There is no detail too small or request too insignificant. In fact, I would suggest the more we bring our requests to God, the more of God's peace we will feel. The other thing I want to point out is that we should go to God with *a thankful heart*. I do not think we are called on to be thankful for the difficulty in and of itself. Instead, we should be thankful

---

[2] KJV.

[3] Read Randy Alcorn's book, *Heaven*, for a glimpse of what Heaven will be like.

that God is with us each and every step of the way, that He is our hope, that we can trust Him, and that He has a plan for us.

1 John 1:9 says that "If we confess our sins, he is faithful and just and will forgive us our sins and purify us from all unrighteousness." God will absolutely forgive us for any sin we've committed. There is no sin that you could have committed that is unforgivable in God's eyes. If you are thinking there is no way you could be forgiven for what you have done, think again. This is a promise from God and He is faithful to fulfill it.

Isaiah 40:31 reads, "but those who hope in the Lord will renew their strength. They will soar on wings like eagles; they will run and not grow weary, they will walk and not be faint." Feeling tired and burned out? Turn to God and put your hope and trust in Him. He will renew your strength. As an aside, I've wondered why God used an eagle in this verse. When I think of a strong animal, an eagle is not the first animal that comes to mind. I'm guessing it's because eagles fly higher than any other birds, and God wanted us to feel the freedom we have in Him. The freedom to soar like an eagle is a picture of hope and strength!

In Isaiah 41, the Lord reminds us, "So do not fear for I am with you; do not be dismayed, for I am your God. I will strengthen you and help you; I will uphold you with my righteous right hand."[4] I shared this verse with a dear friend of mine as he was in the midst of fighting cancer. It helped to get him through this difficult time because of the numerous promises it contains. God is with him, God is his God, God is strengthening him, God is helping him, and God is holding him in the palm of His right hand.

In Jeremiah 29:11, we read, "For I know the plans I have for you declares the Lord, plans to prosper you and not harm you, plans to give you a hope and a future." God promises us here that He has a plan for us that will help us grow and flourish and will not hurt us. The all-knowing, all-powerful, never-changing, loving, and faithful God has a plan for you. Seems to me we should

---

[4] Isaiah 41:10.

take Him up on this promise, no matter where we are in this life. Some may think it's too late. Knowing what we know about God, it's never too late. To fulfill this promise, He will take us where we are and orchestrate our future for our good and His glory as only He can.

Malachi 3:10 says, "'Bring the whole tithe into the storehouse, that there may be food in my house. Test me in this,' says the Lord almighty 'and see if I will not throw open the floodgates of heaven and pour out so much blessing that you will not have enough room for it.'" I've been blessed by the teachings of Pastor Rick Warren of Saddleback Church. One of the things I've heard him say on a number of occasions is that we cannot out-give God. Pastor Rick is not saying that by giving to God, He will absolutely give back to you financially. That may or may not be the case. God promises to bless us beyond all measure, however that may look. Knowing that it is coming from God should be more than enough.

Proverbs 3:5-6 tells us to "Trust in the Lord with all your heart and lean not on your own understanding; in all your ways acknowledge Him, and He will make your path straight." We have often heard it said the shortest path between two points is a straight line. If we want to be the most efficient and get the most done that we can for God, we need to trust the Lord with all that we are and acknowledge Him in all that we do because He is faithful.

Finally, I want to remind you of God's promise in Matthew 11:28-29: "Come to me, all you who are weary and burdened and I will give you rest. Take my yoke upon and learn from me for I am gentle and humble in heart, and you will find rest for your souls." Tired? Burned out? Yeah, I've been there too. For me, it happens when I'm doing things *my* way. Trying to get things done on *my* timeline and forcing *my* agenda. Do you see the word "my" repeatedly in the last sentence? That's the problem.

In the previous chapter, I mentioned that one of the steps to remaining close to God is to slow down. Unfortunately, when I get to the office, I typically go into task mode, e.g., taking care of emails, getting on calls, going to meetings, reviewing work, or visiting clients, often hurrying from one task to the next.

My agenda, my way. My challenge is to slow down, change from a task mode to a relational one, and, most importantly, make room for God in all my interactions at work, at home, at rest, and at play.

It's interesting how I always feel really good doing life God's way, particularly when I am in the office. This requires me to slow down, go at His pace, be present in each conversation, and take whatever time someone needs to resolve something. Not stressing about the outcome, just trusting in God along the way. Doing life God's way always feels better than doing it my way! Whatever tasks need to get done, get done by doing it His way. Most importantly, I honor God in the process, connect with co-workers and clients in a meaningful way, and am not burned out at the end of the day.

God promises to share our burden in a gentle and humble fashion. When we do allow Him to help us, we experience rest because we are choosing to walk with Him at His pace. What is interesting is that when we share our burden with Him, we, too, become gentle and humble in heart. God's example of perfect gentility and humility cannot help but influence us and cause us to behave the same way to those around us when we are yoked to Him and walking by His side. Why I keep going back to "my way," I'll never know.

These promises just scratch the surface. There are thousands more promises from God in the Bible. You can take each and every one of them to the bank because He is faithful. In other words, you can believe His promises are true and return to them for comfort, encouragement, and to remind you of the truth when times are tough. Unlike human parents who sometimes fail to come through, He never fails. He may not work on our timeline, but He always works everything out for our good and His glory when we earnestly seek Him.[5]

His promises are true!

---

[5] Romans 8:28.

Questions:

- Have you ever experienced a broken promise? What happened? How did you feel?

- Have you ever called on one of God's promises? If so, which one and what happened?

- Do you believe God can be relied on to fulfill all His promises? Why or why not?

Mark Chao

8

GOD IS PURE (HOLY)

"There is no one holy like the Lord; there is no one besides you; there is no Rock like our God." (1 Samuel 2:2)

"Your ways, O God are holy. What god is so great as our God?" (Psalm 77:13)

"Holy holy holy is the Lord Almighty; the whole earth is full of His glory." (Isaiah 6:3)

"Yet you are enthroned as the Holy One, you are the praise of Israel." (Psalm 22:3)

"For God did not call us to be impure, but to live a holy life." (1 Thessalonians 4:7)

"Such a high priest meets our need – one who is holy, blameless, pure, set apart from sinners, exalted above the heavens. Unlike the other high priests, he does not need to offer sacrifices day after day, first for his own sins, and then for the sins of the people. He sacrificed for their sins once for all when he offered himself." (Hebrews 7:26-27)

"Great and marvelous are your deeds, Lord God Almighty. Just and true are your ways, King of the ages. Who will fear you, O Lord, and bring glory to your name? For you alone are holy. All nations will come and worship before you, for your righteous acts have been revealed." (Revelation 15:4)

"Holy holy holy is the Lord God Almighty, who was, and is, and is to come." (Revelation 4:8)

God's holiness is mentioned time and again throughout the Bible and is sung about in countless worship songs. Webster's Dictionary defines "holy" as "exalted or worthy of complete devotion as one perfect in goodness and righteousness."[1] The Hebrew word for "holy" is *chodesh*. Chodesh is defined as "apartness, sacredness, or separateness."[2] Both of these definitions are extremely helpful in describing God's holiness.

Twice the Bible uses the phrase "Holy holy holy" in reference to God. Isaiah 6:3 states, "Holy holy holy is the Lord Almighty; the whole earth is full of His glory." And Revelation 4:8 tells us, "Holy holy holy is the Lord God Almighty, who was, and is, and is to come."

Sometimes people repeat a word multiple times to emphasize something. For example, one might use a phrase like "that was a big big house" to emphasize the house's size or "she is a close close friend" to note the closeness of a friendship. "Holy holy holy" is used in a similar manner. It tells us that not only is God holy, but that His holiness is so important it must be emphasized.

Why is God's holiness important? Consider what it would be like if God were not pure and holy. This would mean that God would be capable of performing evil acts. The thought of this is frightening and shakes security in who He is. Could God be trusted? Would you or I be the target of His evil act? This would be like trusting someone who had betrayed you. Furthermore, if God could be evil, there would not be a clear standard by which to live our lives. Would we, too, be free to perform evil acts? Finally, if God were not pure and holy, Jesus could not have been sent to the cross as a pure and unblemished sacrifice for our sins. Thankfully, this is not the case and God is holy.

We encounter God's holiness in Leviticus, chapter 16. God directed the Israelites to, once a year, observe the Day of Atonement (also known as Yom

---

[1] "Holy," Merriam-Webster.com, accessed December 12, 2022, https://www.merriam-webster.com/dictionary/holy.
[2] "Holy, Bible Definition," What Christians Want to Know.com, accessed December 12, 2022, https://www.whatchristianswanttoknow.com/what-is-the-biblical-definition-of-holy/.

Kippur). The purpose behind Yom Kippur was to atone for sins. In the Jewish faith, this is the holiest day of the year. On Yom Kippur, the high priest could enter the Holy of Holies. The Holy of Holies was contained in the Tabernacle. God, in the Book of Exodus, gave very detailed instructions as to how the Tabernacle and Holy of Holies were to be constructed. Once in the Holy of Holies, the high priest would literally be in God's presence.[3]

Entering the Holy of Holies was not to be taken lightly. To enter the Holy of Holies, the high priest had to walk through a curtain that separated the Holy of Holies from the rest of the temple. The high priest had to carefully prepare himself to enter the Holy of Holies by bathing himself and wearing sacred garments. He also had to bring a bull and two goats. Tradition says a rope was tied around the ankle of the high priest when he entered the Holy of Holies in case the high priest did not conduct himself properly. That way, he could be dragged out if something went wrong and he was struck down dead. In Exodus 28:35, we read that Aaron, the first high priest, was commanded to wear special bells on his robe. If the bells stopped ringing, those outside the Holy of Holies would know that something had gone wrong. Two of the high priest's sons died because they treated God's commands with contempt.[4] They were consumed with fire.

On the Day of Atonement, the high priest was required to sacrifice a bull and one of the goats and sprinkle the blood of each on the altar. The high priest would then lay hands on the live goat and confess over it all the wickedness and rebellion of the Israelites there by putting the sins on the goat's head. The high priest would then send the goat into the desert. The goat became the scapegoat for all the confessed sins (and yes, this requirement led to the word "scapegoat"). All this was done to atone for the sins that had been committed by the Jewish people over the past year.

---

[3] Chapter 6 focused on God's omnipresence. The fact that God was present in the Holy of Holies does not mean that He was not still everywhere. Rather, His presence was manifest in the Holy of Holies.

[4] Leviticus 10.

This sacrifice was no longer required after Jesus became the ultimate sacrifice for our sins when He died on the cross. Jesus is holy, and He was holy during His 33 years on this earth. He did not sin. Not once. Because of His holy, sinless life, *Jesus and only Jesus* could pay the ultimate sacrifice for the sins of all, past, present, and future.

While on the cross, Jesus paid for every sin that has ever or will ever be committed. Jesus' sacrificial death on the cross is what allows for our salvation and eternal life with Him in heaven. His crucifixion was the fulfillment of God's plan to save us. It was the ultimate Day of Atonement. No longer do we have to sacrifice bulls or goats to have our sins forgiven. No longer do we have to confess our sins over a scapegoat every year. Rather, we can now confess our sins directly to God and know without a doubt that He has forgiven us.[5]

Jesus paid the ultimate sacrifice for our sins through His sacrifice on the cross. At the moment of Jesus' death, the curtain separating the Holy Place from the Holy of Holies was torn from top to bottom. The curtain could only have torn from top to bottom if God had done this. Think about it: Had man torn the curtain, it would have torn from bottom to top. The significance of the torn curtain is that Jesus' death on the cross opened up access to our Holy holy holy God. The many requirements to enter God's presence in the Holy of Holies were lifted. (We will discuss the Trinity and Holy Spirit more in Chapter 9 but know that the moment you become a believer and receive the forgiveness and mercy of Jesus, the Holy Spirit will began to dwell within you.) God still remains separate and apart (holy), but at the same time, we have direct access to Him as opposed to once a year sending in a priest to atone for our sins.

The significance of God's holiness is that He is still and always will be separate and apart from us because He is God, but through Jesus we have a way to Him. Second, as a Holy God, He is perfect in goodness and righteousness. The opposite of goodness and righteousness is wickedness and evil. Let me pose a question to you: Would you trust someone that is good and righteous or

---

[5] 1 John 1:9.

someone that is wicked and evil? The answer is obvious, and thankfully our God is the former, always and forever.

Let's take a moment to combine God's holiness with his other attributes. His holiness is eternal because He is infinite, and He cannot and will not do anything wicked or evil, ever, because His holiness is perfect and never-changing. There is a famous quote from Lord Acton in which he wrote, "Power tends to corrupt and absolute power corrupts absolutely."[6] We can take comfort in knowing that our all-powerful God cannot be corrupted and that He is truly worthy of our worship and praise.

Questions:

- Have you ever witnessed someone using their power for evil? How about for good?

- How would you define holiness?

- Are you comforted by God's holiness? Why or why not?

- What concerns would you have if God were not holy?

---

[6] Lord Acton, "Power and Authority," Acton.org, accessed December 12, 2022, https://www.acton.org/research/lord-acton-quote-archive.

9

GOD IS THE TRINITY
(FATHER, SON, AND HOLY SPIRIT)

"In the beginning was the Word, and the Word was with God and the Word was God." (John 1:1)

"When the day of Pentecost came, they were all together in one place. Suddenly a sound like the blowing of a violent wind came from heaven and filled the whole house where they were sitting. They saw what seemed to be the tongues of fire that separated and came to rest on each of them. All of them were filled with the Holy Spirit and began to speak in other tongues as the Spirit enabled them." (Acts 2:1-4)

"In the last days, God says, I will pour out my Spirit on all people." (Acts 2:17)

"As soon as Jesus was baptized, he went up out of the water. At that moment heaven was opened and he saw the Spirit of God descending like a dove and alighting him. And a voice from heaven said, 'This is my Son, whom I love; with him I am well pleased.'" (Matthew 3:16-17)

"Therefore go and make disciples of all nations baptizing them in the name of the Father and of the Son and of the Holy Spirit." (Matthew 28:19)

"May the grace of the Lord Jesus Christ, and the love of God, and the fellowship of the Holy Spirit be with you all." (2 Corinthians 13:14)

There are a number of "mysteries" in the world. Mysteries such as the Bermuda Triangle, the Egyptian Pyramids, Stonehenge, and the collapse of the Mayan civilization.

I can remember traveling to Bermuda in the mid-70s as a child. This was at a time when there was significant interest and coverage of the Bermuda Triangle. Why did so many boats sink and planes go down in this part of the Atlantic Ocean? A passenger on the flight was reading a book on the Bermuda Triangle. I recall being a little nervous and wondering why someone would want to read a book on the subject, as we were literally flying over it. Needless to say, I survived.

The mystery behind the Egyptian Pyramids lies in how they were built. How were they able to move stones that weighed several tons many, many miles, and then set them on top of each other? The mystery surrounding Stonehenge isn't how it was built but why it was built. What is the purpose behind all those stones standing in a circle? Finally, what caused such a vibrant society like the ancient Mayans to "suddenly" collapse?

Over time, some of these mysteries have been solved. According to the website HowStuffWorks, the mysteries of the Egyptian Pyramids, the Bermuda Triangle, and the collapse of the Mayan civilization all have rational explanations.[1] However, even with some of the most famous mysteries solved, there are countless others that leave people wondering how in the world they occur. Some will be solved in time, and others will remain mysteries forever.

I would submit the biggest mystery in the world is that of the Holy Trinity, God the Father, God the Son, and God the Holy Spirit. How is it that God can be one entity and three entities all at the same time? This is one mystery we won't fully understand while on this side of Heaven.

With that in mind, I would like to focus on how one can know the Trinity exists, even if we will never understand how it exists. There is ample evidence in the Bible of the Holy Trinity being one (God) and three (Father, Son, and Holy Spirit) all at the same time. Let's start with Isaiah 64:8, "Yet, O Lord,

---

[1] "9 Unsolved Mysteries that have been solved," How Stuff Works, accessed January 30, 2023, https://science.howstuffworks.com/science-vs-myth/unexplained-phenomena/10-unsolved-mysteries-that-have-been-solved.htm.

you are our Father. We are the clay, you are the potter; we are all the work of your hand." This is a clear reference to God the Father.

John 1:1 says, "In the beginning was the Word, and the Word was with God, and the Word was God." The "Word" in this Scripture references Jesus. The "Word" as used here is a clear reference to Jesus as that is John's subject in his gospel. From this, we can conclude Jesus has always been with God and that Jesus also is God.

Peter, in Acts 2:17 (quoting the book of Joel), said, "In the last days, God says, I will pour out *My Spirit* on all people." This is a clear reference to the Holy Spirit being God. 2 Corinthians 3:17 confirms the Spirit being God and reads as follows: "Now the Lord is the *Spirit*, and where the Spirit of the Lord is, there is freedom."[2] I can remember doing word problems in math, and whenever the word "is" was used, I was taught to substitute an equal sign. Applying this to the above scriptures, we get "Lord = Spirit." Through this, we know that God is also the Holy Spirit.

If we link all these verses (Isaiah 64:8, John 1:1, Acts 2:17, and 2 Corinthians 3:17), we can confidently conclude that God is the Father, the Son, and the Holy Spirit, the Trinity. There are many more verses that similarly support the Holy Trinity, including scriptural examples where we read about the Trinity all at once. In Matthew 3, we read the account of Jesus' baptism by John the Baptist. As Jesus came out of the water, the Spirit of God, like a dove, descended on Jesus, and God the Father said, "This is my Son, whom I love; with him I am well pleased."[3] We clearly see the Trinity in this beautiful moment.

In the Great Commission (Matthew 28:19), Jesus tells us, "Therefore go and make disciples of all nations, baptizing them in the name of the Father and of

---

[2] ESV, emphasis added.
[3] Matthew 3:17.

the Son and of the Holy Spirit, and teaching them to obey everything I have commanded you."

In 2 Corinthians 13:14, Paul, in his benediction, writes, "May the grace of the Lord Jesus Christ, and the love of God, and the fellowship of the Holy Spirit be with you all."

One of the things we know about God is that He is always consistent with His teachings. The first of the Ten Commandments tells us we shall have no other gods before God. In the Great Commission, Jesus tells us to baptize in the name of the Father, the Son, and the Holy Spirit. The Trinity is three in one. Jesus wanted to emphasize the triune nature of the Trinity by commanding us to be baptized under three distinct names. However, because they are one, we are able to perfectly obey the first commandment. This similarly explains Paul's benediction where he mentions each member of the Trinity.

Each part of the Trinity has a unique role in God's perfect plan. Jesus and the Holy Spirit will be discussed here including certain aspects of each. Chapter 12 is devoted to God the Father. For now, it is enough to say that God is a good and perfect Father.

As for Jesus, first and foremost, He is the Savior of the world. He lived a sinless life and sacrificed Himself on the cross for our sins because He loved us and was obedient to the Father. Jesus also gave us many incredible teachings through His sermons and interactions and taught us many lessons by the example He set with His actions. His teaching and actions were counter-cultural then and now.

I love His example of servant leadership. In Matthew 20:26-28, Jesus tells us that "whoever wants to become great among you must be your servant, and whoever wants to be first must be your slave—just as the Son of Man did not come to be served, but to serve, and to give his life as a ransom for many." Throughout the four gospels, time and again, we see Jesus serving others up to and through His death on the cross.

I recently read an anonymous quote on Instagram that said, "If you're not ready to serve, you're not ready to lead." I would further define "leadership" as someone who is willing to make sacrifices and put the needs of others before their own. One of the most memorable acts of servant leadership I've witnessed in the business world occurred when I was working for Arthur Andersen. Unfortunately, due to the Enron debacle, Arthur Andersen was being broken apart, and numerous groups of professionals were trying to figure out their next opportunity. Mike Puntoriero, the Orange County Office Managing Partner, was negotiating a transaction to bring most of the Orange County Office to another firm. The initial negotiations called for Mike to be the Orange County Office Managing Partner for this other firm. Midway through the negotiation, Mike was told that, for reasons beyond his control, he could not join this new firm. Regardless, Mike continued to negotiate the transaction to bring clients and professionals to this firm. He successfully completed the transaction and then stepped away. Wow! He had nothing to gain other than to take care of those around him. He could have walked away when he found out that he was no longer part of the deal, but he didn't. Know that there was a happy ending as Mike went on to become the CFO for a couple of very large companies.

There is another side to Jesus we have yet to see. It is one that comforts and causes fear at the same time. The Apostle John in the Book of Revelation describes Jesus as our Warrior King about to do battle:

I saw heaven standing open and there before me was a white horse, whose rider is called Faithful and True. With justice he judges and makes war. His eyes are like blazing fire, and on his head are many crowns. He has a name written on him that no one knows but he himself. He is dressed in a robe dipped in blood, and his name is the Word of God. The armies of heaven were following him, riding on white horses and dressed in fine linen, white and clean. Out of his mouth comes a sharp sword with which to strike down the nations. "He will rule them with an iron scepter." He treads the winepress of the fury of the wrath of God Almighty. On his robe and on his thigh he has this name written: KING OF KINGS AND LORD OF LORDS.[4]

There are paintings of Jesus on the cross, guiding sheep, or sitting with children. The picture painted in Revelation shows the power that Jesus possesses and that paralyzes with fear. Because Jesus is omnipotent (all-powerful), we can know with absolute certainty that He will win this battle.

As Jesus was preparing His disciples for what was to come, He promised them he would send the Holy Spirit. In John 14:16-17, we read, "And I will ask the Father and he will give you another Counselor to be with you forever—the Spirit of truth. The world cannot accept him, because it neither sees him nor knows him. But you know him, for he lives with you and will be in you." Just as with the disciples, God gives us the Holy Spirit when we become followers of Jesus. In fact, the Holy Spirit lives in you if you are a Christian. Yes, God literally lives inside of you. Paul, in 1 Corinthians 6:19, writes, "Do you not know that your body is a temple of the Holy Spirit who is in you, whom you have received from God?" As Paul notes, our bodies are temples of the Holy Spirit.

In Acts 2, we read about God sending the Holy Spirit to the disciples. Immediately, the disciples started speaking in tongues and subsequently began to perform miracles.

If we think back to God's attributes, He is present everywhere. Because of this, we can know that the Holy Spirit resides in each and every believer, consistent with God's attributes. When we abide in the Spirit, when we are mindful of Him in our daily lives, when we put Him first and foremost in our daily activities, we exhibit the fruits of the Spirit: love, joy, peace, patience, kindness, goodness, faithfulness, gentleness, and self-control.[5]

---

[4] Revelation 19:11-16.
[5] Galatians 5:22-23.

Unfortunately, the Holy Spirit seems to get the least attention of the Trinity. The Holy Spirit gets so little attention that Francis Chan wrote a book on the Holy Spirit called *Forgotten God*. Francis believes that many churches have not done enough to focus on the Spirit and explains how and why we need to refocus on the third member of the Trinity. This is a great read, especially if one wants to learn more about the Holy Spirit.

The Holy Spirit fulfills many purposes, some of which are noted here.

The Holy Spirit fills our hearts with God's love. Romans 5:5 states, "And this hope will not lead to disappointment. For we know how dearly God loves us, because [He] has given us the Holy Spirit to fill our hearts with his love."[6] What an incredible truth to know that God's never-ending love is available to us and within us. So, when Jesus tells us to love our neighbors as ourselves, we can do so knowing we can love others and not be concerned about having a limited supply to give away. In fact, I would submit the opposite is true. The more love we give away, the more love we will be supplied with.

The Holy Spirit teaches us all things and reminds us of what Jesus said. In John 14:26, Jesus tells the disciples, "...the Helper, the Holy Spirit, whom the Father will send in my name, he will teach you all things and bring to your remembrance all that I have said to you."[7] If you've ever felt clarity when you read through the Bible or listened to a message, that was the Holy Spirit teaching you. If you've ever been reminded of Jesus' teachings when working through a situation, that was the Holy Spirit bringing that thought to mind.

The Holy Spirit also guides us to the truth. In John 16:13, Jesus tells the disciples, "When the Spirit of truth comes, he will guide you into all the truth, for he will not speak on his own authority, but whatever he hears he will speak, and he will declare to you the things that are to come."[8] The next time you

---

[6] NLT.

[7] ESV.

[8] Ibid.

discover a biblical truth, remember it was the Holy Spirit revealing that truth to you.

Through the Father, the Son, and the Holy Spirit, we get to experience the love of God. I love how the Trinity is described in the NIV footnote to 2 Corinthians 13:14. "The benediction is Trinitarian in form and has ever since been a part of Christian worship tradition. It serves to remind us that the mystery of the Holy Trinity is known to be true not through rational or philosophical explanation but through Christian experience, whereby the believer knows firsthand the grace, the love, and the fellowship that freely flow to him through the three Persons of the one Lord God."[9]

Have you ever felt God the Father's loving arms around you in a difficult time? Have you watched a beautiful sunset that you know He put there just for you? Have you experienced the Father's unexplainable peace during a turbulent time? Have you ever experienced the complete and guilt-free forgiveness of your sins because of what Jesus did on the cross for us? Have you felt the warmth and joy from following Jesus' example by putting others' interests ahead of yours and serving them? Have you felt the Holy Spirit guide you or heard the Spirit's still, quiet voice speaking to you when you are in the middle of making a decision? Or have you had the Spirit open your eyes to one of God's truths? If your answer is yes to any of the above, you have experienced an aspect of the Trinity.

If you haven't experienced these things, please know that God is waiting patiently to shower you with these and many other blessings when we make room for Him by slowing down and patiently seeking His guidance through prayer, studying His Word, and obtaining input from trusted brothers and sisters in Christ.

The Holy Trinity, what a wonderful truth and what an incredible mystery!

---

[9] *NIV Study Notes*, 1996, 1779.

Questions:

- Do you struggle with the concept of the Holy Trinity? If so, how? If not, why?

- Have you ever experienced God in any of the ways noted in the questions above?

- Have you ever experienced servant leadership? If so, what were the circumstances?

10

GOD IS GRACIOUS AND MERCIFUL

"But because of His great love for us, God, who is rich in mercy, made us alive with Christ even when we were dead in transgressions—it is by grace we are saved." (Ephesians 2:4-5)

"For it is by grace you have been saved, through faith—and this not from yourselves, it is the gift of God." (Ephesians 2:8)

"...As far as the east is from the west, so far has He removed our transgressions from us." (Psalm 103:12)

"No matter how deep the stain of your sins, I can take them out and make you clean as freshly fallen snow." (Isaiah 1:18, Living Bible)

"If we confess our sins, He is faithful and just and will forgive us our sins and purify us from all unrighteousness." (1 John 1:9)

When I think of my paternal grandparents, Calvin and Faith Chao, I think of grace. My grandparents were evangelists in China and experienced God's grace on a number of occasions. They founded Inter-Varsity Christian Fellowship chapters at 40 college campuses in China during the 1940s. This was the period when communism was taking a violent foothold in China, putting my grandparents, my dad, and aunts and uncles at risk. My grandparents shared many dramatic stories with me about how God protected them from the Japanese during World War II, the communists, and various mishaps throughout their ministry.

In 1941, my grandparents, along with my dad and aunt, were traveling in a truck through the interior of China when the truck rolled over. My grandma was thrown from the truck but miraculously had no injuries (and she was pregnant with my uncle!). My dad and aunt were fine, and my grandpa only suffered a cut on his face. Unfortunately, many others in the truck suffered serious injuries, and some even died. God mercifully protected them.

On another occasion, during World War II, my grandparents and family were traveling by boat to Shanghai with two American missionaries and other Chinese passengers. Japanese soldiers boarded their boat, and the officer ordered all Chinese passengers to be arrested. Through divine intervention, the officer changed his mind and let my grandparents and family go while arresting the other Chinese passengers on the boat.

When the communist party took over China, my grandpa was informed by a communist friend that he was number three or four on the communist Chinese blacklist because of his and my grandmother's efforts to share the Gospel. If caught, they would have been put in a concentration camp. Once again, God protected them.

In 1948, my grandparents were forced to flee China and came to the United States in 1956 after staying in Hong Kong and Singapore. This came at a time when the United States was only allowing a very limited number of Chinese immigrants per year. My grandparents and aunts and uncles were divinely allocated ten of these slots. Once in the United States, they founded Chinese for Christ, focusing on Chinese missions in the U.S., and established churches in Los Angeles, New York, Chicago, Hayward, Berkeley, and San Jose. In fact, my grandmother was named Woman of the Year by the Los Angeles chapter of the Organization of Chinese American Women for her scholastic achievements and service to the community" when she was 83 years old.[1]

I'm so thankful for my grandpa. He led me to the Lord as a ten-year-old child. I remember one occasion when I experienced my grandpa's grace and, by extension, God's grace. He had experienced a minor stroke, and I went to visit

---

[1] Shawn Maree Smith, "Faith Chao has evangelized from Shanghai to Los Angeles, and at 83 still has big plans. - Los Angeles Times," LATimes.com, accessed December 14, 2022, https://www.latimes.com/archives/la-xpm-1988-11-24-ga-446-story.html.

him in the hospital. I was just out of college at the time, and I was not living a very godly life. He asked me how my walk with Christ was going. I answered honestly, "Grandpa, it's not really what it should be."

I thought he would be disappointed in me, but he looked at me with kind eyes and said, "Don't worry, it will be."

I have thought about this exchange many times and the simple grace he showed and how it gently affected the rest of my life. It was such a wonderful extension of grace with encouragement built in.

I have such fond memories of my grandma, especially her cooking including her fried dumplings. Every time I saw her, she would tell me that she prayed for me every day. At the time, this didn't really mean much to me. As time has passed, I've come to realize that this was so special and how much she blessed and loved me. *My grandma prayed for me every day without fail.* To know that I was covered in prayer means so much to me now, and I'm convinced those prayers kept me from going off the deep end and eventually brought me back to the Lord.

Whenever I hear the song "Amazing Grace," I think of my grandma as that was her favorite hymn. At big family gatherings, she would lead the family in singing this song. It was so off-key and so beautiful. Suffice it to say, I've been blessed with an incredible spiritual heritage along with the experience of God's grace.

I have heard it said that grace is someone giving you something you do not deserve, and mercy is someone removing a punishment you do deserve. When I think of God's forgiveness and promise of eternal life, I think it's a combination of His never-ending never-changing grace and mercy. Ephesians 2:4-5 tells us, "But because of His great love for us, God, who is rich in mercy, made us alive with Christ even when we were dead in transgressions—it is by grace you have been saved." We only have to look at God's actions to appreciate and understand His grace and mercy.

God, through the sacrifice of His Son Jesus Christ on the cross, has given us eternal life with Him in Heaven. This is a gift of grace we definitely do not deserve. Ephesians 2:8 states, "For it is by grace you have been saved, through faith—and this not from yourselves, it is the gift of God..." The grace and the gift are from God. There is nothing we can do to earn them.

At the same time, God has mercifully forgiven all our sins, past, present, and future. Some people may think there is no way God can forgive them for the things they have done. This is a lie. Psalm 103:12 says, "…as far as the east is from the west, so far has He removed our transgressions from us." In the same vein, Isaiah 1:18 tells us, "No matter how deep the stain of your sins, I can take them out and make you clean as freshly fallen snow."[2] Finally, 1 John 1:9 says, "If we confess our sins, He is faithful and just and will forgive us our sins and purify us from all unrighteousness." His grace and mercy abound.

He has forgiven our sins and taken away the everlasting consequences of them through the death and resurrection of Jesus. As we read in 1 Peter 1:3, "Praise be to the God and Father of our Lord Jesus Christ. In His great mercy, He has given us new birth into a living hope through the resurrection of Jesus Christ from the dead."

Let there be no doubt that God will forgive all our sins, no matter what we've done. However, God may not remove the consequences of our sins. He has given us free will. Our decisions and actions lead to natural outcomes. We reap what we sow. Typically, good decisions lead to good consequences, and bad decisions lead to bad outcomes. In fact, Proverbs 13:15 tells us, "Good judgment wins favor, but the way of the unfaithful leads to their destruction." Some may argue that God allows negative consequences because He is angry and wants to punish us. But, as we now know, God is a God of love who wants nothing but the best for us. Like a loving parent, God may allow us to suffer certain consequences because He wants to encourage us to do the right thing the next time around.

---

[2] Living Bible.

If we suffer a difficult consequence as the result of a bad decision we've made, know that God doesn't delight in our suffering. Rather, He allows us to go through what we must go through to learn what we must learn while preserving our free will. This is rooted in His incredible love for you and me and His desire to protect us from destruction.

At this point, I want to consider what Jesus went through on His way to and on the cross. Some might say that what Jesus suffered on the cross was no big deal because He is God, a cheap grace of sorts. This couldn't be further from the truth. Consider the following:

- Jesus knew what He was going to suffer was going to be excruciating. Jesus did not want to go through with it. Twice He asks God to find another way if possible, yet Jesus concludes that God's will be done.[3]

- Jesus literally sweated blood.[4] Sweating blood is a rare medical condition known as **hematohidrosis**. According to WebMD, it can be caused by extreme distress or fear, such as facing death, torture, or severe ongoing abuse.[5] We've all faced incredibly stressful situations, but I doubt it caused us to sweat blood. Clearly, Jesus experienced severe stress and anxiety leading up to the crucifixion.

- In the various Biblical accounts of the crucifixion, we read that Jesus was humiliated and beaten by the Roman guards. They spat on Him, repeatedly struck Him, and put a crown of thorns on Him.[6]

- Jesus was flogged.[7] A flog is not just a whip. A flog is a whip with multiple strands, and tied to the strands were pieces of bone and lead. Each strike resulted in deep bruising and cuts. The typical flogging consisted of 39 strikes, as 40 strikes would cause death.

---

[3] See Matthew 26:39 and 26:42.

[4] Luke 22:44.

[5] "Hematidrosis (Sweating Blood): Symptoms, Causes, Treatment (webmd.com)," WebMD, accessed January 30, 2023, https://www.webmd.com/a-to-z-guides/hematidrosis-hematohidrosis#1.

[6] Mark 15; Matthew 27; Luke 23; John 19.

[7] John 19:1.

- Crucifixion was a brutal way to die. The person being crucified literally suffers a slow suffocation. Nails are pounded into the hands and feet. In order to breathe, the person on the cross must lift themselves up by putting pressure on their hands and feet and suffer excruciating pain because of the nails. The very act of breathing resulted in agonizing pain. Crucifixions typically took hours and hours. Eventually, the person on the cross quits raising themselves up to breathe, and they suffocate. What I find incredible is that Jesus had the wherewithal to forgive a man while He was on the cross. There were two criminals that were crucified with Jesus. One of the criminals hurled insults at Jesus. The other criminal rebuked him and said that we are being punished justly but this man (Jesus) has done nothing wrong. He then says "Jesus, remember me when you come into your kingdom." Jesus replied to him "I tell you the truth, today you will be with me in paradise."[8] Talk about grace and mercy.

- Jesus bore the sins of all on the cross. As He did this, I have a visual of all our sins as an incredibly foul sludge being poured through a filter, Jesus. He is literally bearing every sin, past, present, and future. After passing through Jesus, I envision pure, pristine water coming out the other side. As this is happening, Jesus cries out, "My God, my God, why have you forsaken me?"[9] Why? Because at this moment, God had to abandon Jesus. God is pure and holy and had to separate Himself from Jesus as Jesus paid for our sins. I think of all the things that Jesus suffered, this was the most painful and distressing, more than the physical punishment He dealt with. Remember that Jesus had always been with God and had never been separated from Him up to that point. The pain and anguish this caused Jesus is evidenced by Jesus' cry. At no point throughout Jesus' trial, beating, and crucifixion do we hear Him complain or say anything about His physical suffering. Only at the moment when God is forced to turn His back on Jesus and pour out His wrath on Him do we hear Jesus cry out,

---

[8] Luke 23:40-43.
[9] Matthew 27:46.

"My God, My God, why have you forsaken me?" Thankfully, the one thing that Jesus dreaded the most will never happen to us because we know God has PROMISED never to leave or forsake us.

I have always focused on Jesus' crucifixion and what he suffered, but I recently started to wonder what God the Father went through. As a dad, I would never want to see my kids suffer. Earlier, I mentioned the story of Jim Zorn and how he would sacrifice himself before his children. Yet, God loves us so much that He sacrificed His Son and had to endure watching Jesus suffer. Imagine the moment when Jesus is crying out to Him. God had literally turned His back on Jesus, and Jesus knew it. As a dad, I think God heard, "Papa, papa, where are you? Please help me!" That would tear me up inside, and I would feel like my heart was being ripped out. I can only imagine that it did the same to God. Yes, He is God, but He is also Jesus' Papa. I believe it wasn't only Jesus that suffered. Remember, God the Father could have stopped this with the snap of a finger, but He, too, endured this for us. That is how much God loves you and me and is another example of His grace and mercy.

Jesus suffered all these things because of His love for each and every one of us. There was nothing cheap or easy about what He went through for us to show us grace and mercy. To experience God's grace and mercy, all we have to do is accept Jesus Christ as our Lord and Savior. It is then that all our sins are forgiven, and true inner peace is possible. Know that nothing you have ever done or will do will be held against you by God when you submit to the Lordship of His Son. Whatever guilt you may be holding from prior transgressions can be released. God sees you as pure as a result of Jesus' sacrifice on the cross. At this point, I ask you to pause and experience God's incredible peace that emanates from His gift of salvation.

The crucifixion story is not complete, though, unless we include His resurrection from the grave on the third day.[10] On the third day, Mary Magdalane and another Mary went to Jesus' tomb. An angel of the Lord

---

[10] If you want to see a depiction of what Jesus went through, I would suggest you watch Mel Gibson's "The Passion of the Christ."

appeared to them and told them "Do not be afraid, for I know that you are looking for Jesus who was crucified. He is not here; he has risen, just as he said." [11] He is risen indeed.

Questions:

- Have you ever experienced the forgiveness of someone you wronged? How did it make you feel the moment they forgave you?

- Have you ever struggled with forgiving someone? Why?

- Have you experienced God's forgiveness?

- Are there any sins you've committed that you continue to feel guilty about? If so, why do you continue to feel guilty?

---

[11] Matthew 28:1-6

11

GOD IS SOVEREIGN/GREAT

"O house of Israel, can I not do with you as this potter does?" declares the Lord. "Like clay in the hand of the potter, so are you in my hand." (Jeremiah 18:6, ESV)

"I am God and there is no other; I am God and there is none like me. I make known the end from the beginning, from ancient times, what is still to come. I say, 'My purpose will stand, and I will do all that I please.'" (Isaiah 46:9-10)

The book of Esther tells the dramatic story of the King of Persia, Xerxes, and the events that followed his marriage to a woman named Esther. The story begins with Xerxes searching for a new wife and queen because the existing queen, Queen Vashti, disobeyed him. Xerxes issued a decree that all the beautiful women be brought to him so that he could select the new queen. After a protracted process, Xerxes selected Esther. Esther was also the cousin of Mordecai, a high-ranking official in Xerxes' court who, in the past, saved Xerxes' life by unveiling an assassination plot against him.

Subsequent to this, Xerxes was deceived by one of his advisers, Haman, to issue a decree that all the Jews in Persia should be killed in the near future.

In a dramatic twist, Esther was made aware of Haman's plot to kill all the Jews in Persia. Esther herself was Jewish, and she was convinced by her cousin, Mordecai, to approach Xerxes to beg him to stop the genocide. Normally, an audience with the king was at the king's discretion. If a subject presented themselves to the king without being summoned, they risked death. Esther had to be exceptionally brave to present herself to Xerxes without being summoned. Thankfully, Xerxes extended his gold scepter, which meant she could approach. Had he not extended his scepter, she would have been put to death, even as queen.

Esther played her cards carefully and requested that Xerxes and Haman both come to a banquet in her quarters. In the meantime, Xerxes suffered from insomnia and had someone read him the book of the Chronicles, the record of his reign, to pass away the restless night hours. During the story time, Xerxes was reminded that Mordecai foiled an assassination plot against him. Xerxes ordered Haman to make sure that Mordecai was honored throughout the city. The irony is that Haman thought *he* was the one to be honored. The very man who wanted to kill all the Jews wound up being commanded to honor one in the way he wished to be honored himself!

Back to the banquet with Xerxes, Haman, and Esther. The king was so pleased with Esther that he promised to honor her request, whatever it was, up to one-half the kingdom. Esther told the king that her people were going to be annihilated. The king, not knowing Esther was Jewish, was furious. Who would dare harm his wife's family with such an evil plot?

The truth comes out that Esther is Jewish and that Haman is behind the whole thing. Xerxes commanded that Haman be hanged. He then gave Haman's estate to Esther and his signet ring to Mordecai, making him the number two person in the kingdom. Finally, Xerxes signed a new decree allowing the Jews to defend themselves and plunder their enemies on the day of destruction. In Esther 8:8, King Xerxes instructed Mordecai, "Now write another decree in the king's name on behalf of the Jews as seems best to you, and seal it with the king's signet ring—for no document written in the king's name and sealed with his ring can be revoked."

Throughout the book of Esther, King Xerxes issued command after command.

- He removed the existing queen.
- He ordered that all the beautiful young women be brought to him.
- He is deceived into issuing a decree that all Jews be killed.

- He allowed Esther to approach him.

- He granted Esther's request for a banquet.

- He ordered that Mordecai be honored for saving his life.

- He ordered that Haman be hanged.

- He ordered that Haman's estate be given to Esther.

- He gave his signet ring to Mordecai and empowered him as the number two person in the kingdom.

- He ordered Mordecai to issue a new decree to protect the Jews from genocide.

Each and every one of these commands and decrees was carried out. Xerxes emphasized his power when he said that any document written in the king's name and sealed with the signet ring could not be revoked. It had to be obeyed. Why was he able to do this? As king of Persia, *Xerxes was sovereign.*

Merriam-Webster defines "sovereign" as one possessing or held to possess supreme political power or sovereignty, one that exercises supreme authority within a limited sphere.[1] Xerxes had supreme authority within the kingdom of Persia. There was no one to tell Xerxes what to do, and the final decisions were left to him. His decisions could, however, be influenced by those around him for good and for evil, as we saw with Haman.

God's sovereignty is absolute. His authority and power are not limited. No one can command God, and His authority and power are unstoppable. In fact, it was God that put Xerxes on the throne. Daniel 2:20-21 says, "He changes times and seasons; he deposes kings and raises up others. He gives wisdom to the wise and knowledge to the discerning." God tells the Israelites in Jeremiah 27:4-5, "Tell this to your masters: with my great power and outstretched arm I made the earth and its people and the animals that are on it, and I give it to

---

[1] "Sovereign," Merriam-Webster.com Dictionary, Merriam-Webster, accessed December 15, 2022, https://www.merriam-webster.com/dictionary/sovereign.

anyone I please." God is able to do whatever pleases Him. No one and nothing controls God. He has ultimate authority.

Unlike Xerxes, God cannot be influenced into making a bad decision. Remember, God is omniscient. He cannot be told something He doesn't already know. God can do ANYTHING He pleases, "I am God and there is no other; I am God and there is none like me. I make known the end from the beginning, from ancient times, what is still to come. I say: My purpose will stand, and I will do all that I please."[2] Remember that God is also all-powerful, and there is nothing that can stand up to God's power. Having said that, we need to combine God's sovereignty with all the other attributes we've read about up until this point. God is holy, God is gracious and merciful, God is loving, and God is faithful. As King of kings and Lord of lords, I'm thankful to have God as my sovereign because He wants nothing but the best for me. He knows what that is and guides me.

Knowing all this, we need to ask ourselves if we actually trust God. If not, who or what are we putting our trust in, and why would we put our trust in anything over a holy, gracious, loving, all-powerful, all-knowing, never-changing, sovereign God that wants the best for us?

Knowing that God is sovereign and wants the best for us, why does He let bad things happen? This is an oft-posed question and one that causes believers and nonbelievers to stumble. The world God created was good. Genesis 1:31 notes that "God saw that all he had made, and it was very good." Knowing what we know about God, He would not have called His creation good if it was not, in fact, good. The sins of Adam and Eve changed this and allowed evil, sickness, and tragedy into the world. The bad things that happen are a consequence of the original sin.

The Bible tells us to expect difficult times. In John 16:33, Jesus tells us, "In this world you will have trouble. But take heart! I have overcome the world." It is our hope in Jesus and the promise of eternal life with Him and our loved

---

[2] Isaiah 46:9-10.

ones that help us get through difficult times. I'm reminded of a sermon I heard that put the troubles in our time here on earth in perspective. The pastor tied a piece of string from one end of the church to the other. I'm guessing it stretched out 150 feet. The long piece of string represented eternity. He placed a bead at the beginning of the string and said this represented our time here on earth. His point was that the troubles we face here on earth are for a very short time. Please know that I am not trying to diminish the difficulties of this life. Seeing loved ones lose a battle with cancer or pass away unexpectedly brings on incredible grief. At the same time, we have the hope of seeing these same loved ones who believed in Jesus in Heaven one day with an eternity to reunite.

Sometimes we get frustrated because things do not happen when we want them to. Because God is eternal and infinite, time does not apply to Him. 2 Peter 3:8 states, "With the Lord a day is like a thousand years, and a thousand years are like a day." God is outside time and brings an eternal perspective to all things. He can see the beginning, the middle, and the end. Compare that to our extremely limited perspective. God's plan for the best in our lives and to prosper us includes His timing, not ours. With this in mind, we must trust God's timing.

Lastly, we should be reminded that God walks through these difficult times with us because He is always with us. Not only does He walk through these times with us, but he feels what we feel just as when Jesus wept when Lazarus died. God is not distant or uncaring. He is compassionate, which is consistent with His love for us. There is an old proverb that says, "a sorrow shared is halved and a joy shared is doubled." I firmly believe this also applies to our relationship with Jesus.

If you're wondering how He is able to share in our joys and sorrows, we only need to reflect on God's attributes: He loves us beyond all measure, He knows every detail about us and what we're going through moment by moment, including our thoughts, and He is always with us.

When I was in the midst of my job change (see Foreward), I was interviewing with one of the other major accounting firms to work in their Orange County office. I was scheduled to have lunch with one of their tax partners, Lance Wood. As we walked across the street to the restaurant, Lance's first question to me was, "You're a Christian, aren't you?" For those of you that have conducted interviews, there are certain topics that are off limits, e.g., marital status, whether you have children, political affiliation, age, and religion. I was a little taken aback by the question, but of course, I answered, "Yes."

Lance proceeded to explain to me why he asked the question. The previous Friday, he was picking up his children from Vacation Bible School. He ran into a friend of his, Rick. Turns out Rick was also a friend of mine from high school. (In fact, I had seen Rick a couple of months earlier at our high-school reunion, and we had a chance to catch up.) As they were chatting, Rick asked Lance whether he knew me. Lance said no but that he was having lunch with me the next week, and Rick gave him some background on me. Lance had an inkling that I was the right man for the job, and I took the position soon after.

I mention this little scenario because many people would say all of this was just a coincidence. Knowing what I know about God and all His attributes, including His sovereignty, this was no coincidence. God coordinated all these encounters and showed me He was in control of my situation. His promises to give me peace that surpasses all understanding and to work all things for good were fulfilled.

I was blessed in so many ways through that job. One such blessing was the gift of time. My daily commute went from two to three hours to *30 minutes per day*. Because of this, I was able to have family dinners most nights, coach my kids, and attend almost all their events and activities. This would not have happened had I not been forced to resign and find a new job. The new firm perfectly fit my personality and allowed me to be who I am.

As icing on the cake, Lance and I have maintained a close friendship for almost 25 years, and he and I are accountability partners. As accountability partners, we ask each other the tough questions and encourage each other in our walk with God as husbands and fathers. God, in His sovereignty, orchestrated all of this. He brought good out of a difficult circumstance. He is the master of bringing good out of evil (or even just a less-than-ideal circumstance) if we let Him.

Romans 8:28 reminds us, "...We know that in all things God works for the good of those who love him, who have been called according to his purpose." How is it that God is able to keep this promise? Let's go back to what we know about God: He is all-powerful, all-knowing, ever-present, holy, faithful, and sovereign. Knowing this, we can absolutely have the confidence that God will overcome evil with good. When we get to Heaven, I imagine we'll have a chance to ask Jesus why certain things happened the way they did, and each time He answers, our response will be, "Oh, now I get it."

Not only is God sovereign, He is also great, in fact the greatest. We are reminded of God's greatness throughout the Bible:

- *"Oh, the depth of the riches of the wisdom and knowledge of God! How unsearchable his judgements and his paths beyond tracing out! Who has known the mind of the Lord? Or who has been his counselor? Who has ever given to God, that God should repay him? For from him and through him are all things. To him be the glory forever! Amen." (Romans 11:33-36)*

- *"As the heavens are higher than the earth, so are my ways higher than your ways and my thoughts than your thoughts." (Isaiah 55:9)*

- *"Who can fathom the Spirit of the LORD, or instruct the LORD as his counselor?" (Isaiah 40:13)*

- *"Can you fathom the mysteries of God? Can you probe the limits of the almighty? They are higher than the heavens—what can you do? They are deeper than the depths of the grave --- what can you know? Their measure is longer than the earth and wider than the sea." (Job 11:7-9)*

- *"Great is the Lord and most worthy of praise, his greatness no one can fathom." (Psalm 145:3)*

God's greatness is evidenced by the many prophecies contained in the Bible that have been fulfilled. In Lee Strobel's *The Case for Christ*, he writes about the odds that one man could fulfill all 48 Messianic prophecies. He quotes a study by a mathematician, Peter W. Stoner. Stoner calculated that the probability is one in a trillion, trillion, trillion, trillion, trillion, trillion, trillion, trillion, trillion, trillion, trillion, trillion, trillion. An illustration in Lee's book discusses what it would look like statistically speaking for one man to fulfill just eight messianic prophecies. The probability would be like filling the state of Texas two feet deep with silver dollars and one gold coin. You would then blindfold someone and tell them to reach down and grab the gold coin in one try, and they do!

The fulfillment of prophecies is evidence of God being all-powerful and all-knowing. God told His people what was going to happen in the future through His power and knowledge. These prophecies are a gift from God. God gave us these prophecies and their fulfillment to help us believe in and obey Him. Romans 16:25-26 tells us "Now to him who is able to establish you by my gospel and the proclamation of Jesus Christ, according to the revelation of the mystery hidden for long ages past, but now revealed and made known through the prophetic writings by the command of the eternal God, so that all nations might believe and obey him – to the only wise God be glory forever through Jesus Christ! Amen."

Here is a sample of prophecies that were foretold in the Old Testament and fulfilled in the New Testament primarily through Jesus to help us believe and obey. It's important to note that these Old Testament prophecies were written approximately 600 – 1,000 years before their fulfillment.

Background	Old Testament Prophecy	New Testament Fulfillment
Isaiah prophesized that a virgin would give birth to Jesus. The name Immanuel in Isaiah 7:14 means "God with us." A clear reference to Jesus.	Isaiah 7:14 Therefore the Lord himself will give you a sign: The virgin will be with child and will give birth to a son, and will call him Immanuel.	Luke 1:30-35 But the angel said to her, "Do not be afraid, Mary, you have found favor with God. You will be with child and give birth to a son, and you are to give him the name Jesus. He will be great and will be called the Son of the Most High. The Lord God will give him the throne of his father David, and he will reign over the hour of Jacob forever; his kingdom will never end." "How will this be," Mary asked the angel, "since I am a virgin?" The angel answered "The Holy Spirit will come upon you, and the power of the Most High will overshadow you. So the holy one to be born will be called the Son of God."
Micah prophesized that Jesus would be born in Bethlehem. The fulfillment of this prophecy required that Jesus be born at the time of the	Micah 5:2 But you, Bethlehem Ephrathah, though you are small among the clans of Judah, out of you will come for me one who will be ruler	Luke 2:1-7 In those days Caesar Augustus issued a decree that a census should be taken of the entire Roman world. (This was the first census that took place

Background	Old Testament Prophecy	New Testament Fulfillment
census. When a census was taken, which was only occasionally, individuals were required to be counted in their city of origin.	over Israel, whose origins are from of old, from ancient times.	while Quirinius was governor of Syria.) And everyone went to his own town to register. So Joseph also went up from the town of Nazareth in Galilee to Judea, to Bethlehem the town of David, because he belonged to the house and line of David. He went there to register with Mary, who was pledged to be married to him and was expecting a child. While they were there, the time came for the baby to be born, and she gave birth to her first-born, a son. She wrapped him in cloths and placed him in a manger, because there was no room at the inn.
		Luke 2:1-7 – See above
Jeremiah prophesized that Jesus would come from the line of David. Joseph, Jesus' earthly father, was a descendant of David.	Jeremiah 33:15 In those days and at that time I will make a righteous Branch sprout from David's line; he will do what is just and right in the land.	

Background	Old Testament Prophecy	New Testament Fulfillment
Hosea prophesized that Jesus would come out of Egypt. This is not inconsistent with Jesus being born in Bethlehem as He lived temporarily in Egypt.	Hosea 11:1 "When Israel was a child, I loved him and out of Egypt I called my son.	Matthew 2:13 When they had gone, an angel of the Lord appeared to Joseph in a dream. "Get up" he said, "take the child and his mother and escape to Egypt. Stay there until I tell you, for Herod is going to search for the child to kill him. So he got up, took the child and his mother during the night and left for Egypt, where he stayed until the death of Herod. And so was fulfilled what the Lord had said through the prophet: "Out of Egypt I called my son."
Isaiah prophesized that there would be someone who came before Jesus that would prepare the way for Him. This was fulfilled by John the Baptist.	Isaiah 40:3 A voice of one calling: "In the desert prepare the way for the Lord, make straight in the wilderness a highway for our God."	Mark 1:2-4 It is written in Isaiah the prophet: "I will send my messenger ahead of you, who will prepare your way" – "a voice of one calling in the desert, Prepare the way for the Lord, make straight paths for him." And so John came, baptizing in the desert region and preaching a baptism of

Background	Old Testament Prophecy	New Testament Fulfillment
		repentance for the forgiveness of sins.
It was prophesized that Jesus' hands and feet would be pierced. Crucifixion was a Roman form of execution that required the individual's hands and feet be nailed to a cross. It's important to note that Psalm 22 was written hundreds of years before crucifixion had been invented by the Romans.	Psalm 22:16 Dogs have surrounded me; a band of evil men has encircled me, they have pierced my hands and my feet.	Mark 15:24 And they crucified him. Dividing up his clothes, they cast lots to see what each would get.
It was prophesized that lots would be cast for Jesus' clothes. Casting lots is the modern day equivalent of drawing straws.	Psalm 22:18 They divide my garments among them and cast lots for my clothing	See Mark 15:24 above

Background	Old Testament Prophecy	New Testament Fulfillment
Zechariah prophesized that Jesus would be pierced. When Jesus was crucified, a Roman soldier pierced Jesus' side with a spear to make sure he was dead.	Zechariah 12:10 And I will pour out on the house of David and the inhabitants of Jerusalem a spirit of grace and supplication. They will look on me, the one they have pierced.	John 19:33-35 But when they came to Jesus and found that he was already dead, they did not break his legs. Instead, they pierced Jesus' side with a spear, bringing a sudden flow of blood and water. The man who saw it has given testimony, and his testimony is true. He knows that he tells the truth, and he testifies so that you may also believe.
It was prophesized that none of Jesus' bones would be broken. Often times a Roman soldier would break the legs of the individual on the cross to speed up their death.	Psalm 34:19-20 A righteous man may have many troubles, but the Lord delivers him from them all: he protects all his bones, not one of them will be broken.	See John 19:33-35 above

There are prophecies still yet to be fulfilled, and we know that they will come true. The best prophecy is that we know the end of the story, and God wins!!! There are no coincidences in our lives. We know that God is able to fulfill all His prophecies. And doing so is consistent with who He is.

Questions:

- Considering all of God's attributes, including His sovereignty, do you truly trust God? Why or why not?
- Have you seen God bring good out of bad?
- Do you have an accountability partner? If not, think of someone you could connect with on this deep level.

12

OUR PAPA IN HEAVEN

In this chapter, we will cover God the Father. Before we do that, I would like to recap the attributes of God we have covered:

- God Has Never Changed and Will Never Change
- God Is Infinite and Eternal
- God Is Love
- God Is All-Powerful
- God Knows Everything
- God Is Everywhere
- God Is Faithful
- God Is Pure (Holy)
- God Is The Father, Son, and Holy Spirit
- God Is Gracious and Merciful
- God Is Sovereign/Great

It bears repeating: God has been, is, and will be all these things all the time.

These are things we can know about God, things He has chosen to reveal to us in the Bible and in nature. But to entertain the thought that we know all there is to know about God would, by definition, diminish who He is and would be an unjust elevation of who we are and, arguably, arrogant.

With all these amazing things we know about God, I would now like to take a deeper look at God as Abba, our Father. In the words of Paul in Romans 8:15, "The Spirit you received does not make you slaves, so that you live in fear again; rather, the Spirit you received brought about your adoption to sonship. And by him we cry, 'Abba, Father.'"[1] In his letter to the Galatians, Paul wrote, "Because you are sons, God sent the Spirit of the Son into our hearts, the Spirit who calls out, 'Abba, Father.'"

As believers, we are sons and daughters of God. God is your Father and mine. I'd like to use the word "dad" here, but as I researched the phrase "Abba, Father," using "dad" would be too familiar and would not bring the proper level of respect and authority to God. "Abba, Father" indicates an intimate relationship but also requires appropriate respect and authority. With that in mind, maybe the word "papa" gets us closer.

When someone calls their father "papa," I believe the person saying this has an intimate and loving relationship with their father while also acknowledging they respect and honor their father's authority. So, if you will grant me license, let's go with that. God, the Father, is our Papa in Heaven.

The impact a father has on a child cannot be overstated. I was watching an ESPN special several years ago about a college running back who was adopted. He wanted to find his birth parents. He found his birth mom, and she told him who his birth father was. The crazy thing is, this young man had known his birth father for years without either of them knowing the connection. In fact, his birth father was his football coach and mentor. People often said they looked and acted alike. When they met as father/son for the first time, the coach/now dad called the young man, "My son." The impact of these words on the son was huge. He had never had a man say that to him.

The young man described it like this: "I know he was saying it from a place of 'I'm proud. This is my son.' I'd never heard that before—period. It really hit me hard emotionally. When I sit here at this point, and I'm looking at things that I've done, I'm happy that I'm able to be somebody that he's proud of."

---

[1] ESV.

The desire a child has for a father, even an adult child, is universal. Fathers are vital to the raising of children that become well-adjusted adults. The impact a father, or better yet, the lack of a father, has on a child is reflected in the following statistics.

→ Almost 30% of children live in fatherless homes—19.7 million.[2]

→ 47.6% of fatherless homes live in poverty—four times the rate for two-parent households.[3]

→ Children from fatherless homes account for:

- ◆ 63% of youth suicides.

- ◆ 90% of all homeless and runaway youths.

- ◆ 85% of children who exhibit behavioral disorders.

- ◆ 71% of high-school dropouts.

- ◆ 70% of youths in state institutions.

- ◆ 75% of adolescent patients in substance abuse centers.

- ◆ 85% of rapists that are motivated by displaced anger.[4]

Think about these statistics. Thirty percent of children grow up in fatherless homes, yet they account for 63–90% of the above. The importance of fathers is obvious. Dads, if you want to have a positive impact and leave a legacy, be present. It will be one of the best things you will ever do. If you have been an absent father, prayerfully consider going to your children with humility, with love, with a heartfelt apology, without any expectations, and trust the outcome to God.

---

[2] Census Bureau.

[3] "The Consequences of Fatherlessness," Fathers.com, accessed December 15, 2022, https://fathers.com/the-consequences-of-fatherlessness/.

[4] "What Can the Federal Government Do to Decrease Crime and Revitalize Communities?" January 1998, Department of Health and Human Services. Although this report is a bit dated, it is still frequently cited.

When I think of a good father, I think of someone that:

- Loves
- Listens
- Teaches, guides, and disciplines
- Provides and is generous
- Is consistent
- Sacrifices and is selfless
- Keeps his word
- Is patient
- Is honest
- Makes time and is present
- Forgives
- Protects and defends
- Supports his children
- Shows compassion
- Is joyful

How does God the Father compare to this list?

- Loves – We know God's love is immense and never-ending. (Psalm 107:1)
- Listens – We know God hears our prayers. (1 Peter 3:12)
- Teaches, guides, and disciplines – God teaches us through the Bible and disciplines us with wisdom for our good out of His love for us. (Proverbs 3:11-12)
- Provides and is generous – Every good and perfect gift comes from God. (James 1:17)

- Is consistent – God never changes. (Hebrews 13:8)

- Sacrifices and is selfless – God sent His Son to the cross for us. (Romans 5:10)

- Keeps his word – He is faithful, always keeping His promises. (Deuteronomy 7:9)

- Is patient – God has an eternal perspective. In addition, we know that God is patient because love is patient, and God is love! (1 Corinthians 13:4)

- Is honest – He is pure and holy. (1 Samuel 2:2)

- Makes time and is present – He is infinite and always present. (Psalm 139:7-10)

- Forgives – God has forgiven all our sins, past, present, and future, through Jesus. (1 John 1:9)

- Protects and defends – God protects and defends us. "You are my protector and defender. I put my hope in your promises." (Psalm 119:114, GNT)

- Supports his children – "I will guide you along the best pathway for your life. I will advise you and watch over you." (Psalm 32:8, NLT)

- Shows compassion – "The Lord is gracious and righteous; our God is full of compassion." (Psalm 116:5)

- Joyful – "Be joyful always…for this is God's will for you in Christ Jesus." (1 Thessalonians 5:16) He wants us to be joyful as He is joyful.

It is clear that God possesses all the characteristics of a good father. He is all these things and more. He is the *perfect* Father.

If you grew up or are growing up without an earthly father, I am so sorry. Some, including me, did not have an idyllic father growing up. Unfortunately, this causes many to project the way their father treated them onto God the Father. If your dad was not around or not emotionally or mentally present when he was physically there, you may view God as distant or possibly selfish. If your dad was angry and abusive, you might view God as an angry/abusive God. If your dad was unfaithful or dishonest, you might view God as untrustworthy.

But here is the incredible news. We have a perfect Heavenly Father, Papa, who is with us and loves us now and forevermore! None of the difficulties we faced with our earthly fathers could possibly be the case when it comes to God the Father. He is the one and only perfect Papa. As our Papa, He desires an intimate relationship and wants nothing but the best for us. He is the idyllic Papa that we can place all our trust and hope in, loves us beyond all measure, and is mightier than all. He shouts for joy over you and shares His power and wisdom with you. This Papa is pure, holy, and good always and forever.

There is a story in the Bible that gives us an incredible look at God the Father, the parable of the prodigal son.[5] This parable involves a father with two sons. The younger son goes to the father and says, "Father, give me my share of the estate." This was an insult to the father as he was still alive. Yet, the father gives the son his share of the estate. This son moves to another country and blows it all, living an incredibly wildlife. Later, the son, now destitute, finds work feeding pigs and is so hungry, he wants to eat the same food as what he is feeding the pigs. The son realizes his mistakes and decides to return home to ask his father for forgiveness and for a job as a hired worker. The father sees him coming from a distance and runs to his son to give him a huge hug. The son asks for forgiveness. The father then tells his servants to put the best robe on his son, a ring on his finger, and sandals on his feet. He then orders that the fattened calf be slaughtered, and a banquet held for his son because he "…was dead and is alive again; he was lost and is found."[6]

The son's request of his living dad was highly unusual and disrespectful. Imagine asking someone for your inheritance while that person is still living. Yet, the father was ecstatic to see his son return and ran to him. This is how

---

[5] Luke 15:11-32.
[6] Luke 15:24, KJV.

God the Father feels about us. He runs to us when we return to Him. He throws an incredible party and puts the best clothes on us. Why? Because we were lost, and now, we are found. God the Father does not care what we did previously or that we sinned. *He cares that we are coming back with a heart of repentance.*

If you have walked away from Papa, He is waiting to run to you.

If you do not have a relationship with Papa but want one, it's really pretty simple. All you have to do is accept Jesus as your Savior. You might pray something simple like this: "Papa, I thank You that You sent Jesus to the cross for me. I ask that You forgive all my sins, and I accept Your Son as my Lord and Savior. In Jesus' name, I pray, Amen."

If you prayed this, congratulations and welcome to God's family. Not only are we celebrating with you here on earth, but the angels in heaven are rejoicing over you. Please tell a fellow believer or tell me at markchao85@gmail.com so that we can help you on this amazing adventure with God. If you are hesitating to accept Jesus as your Savior because you think that God will not forgive you for the things you have done, please remember back to the chapter on God's grace and mercy. ANY sin you've committed is absolutely forgiven.

The father I longed for and likely that you are longing for is with you and is always available to you. He wants nothing more than for you to look to Him and the hope that comes to us through our Papa. You may not have had the earthly father you hoped for, but you have the best Father ever, our Papa in Heaven.

Questions

- What is your idea of a perfect father?
- What type of relationship did you have with your father?
- How has it impacted your view of God the Father?

Mark Chao

13

WHAT DOES THIS MEAN TO YOU AND ME?

I struggle to think of a worship song or a sermon that I have heard that did not mention one of God's attributes. The next time you sing a worship song or listen to a sermon, focus on the attribute or attributes at hand. (If God's attributes are not somehow included in the message or the song, or the attributes mentioned are inconsistent with who God is, you will want to examine the content more closely to ensure the message is biblically true.) Then, think about the other attributes you know to be true about God and how they magnify and intertwine with the attribute(s) at hand. For example, when you hear that God loves you, remember that His love is eternal and beyond anything we could comprehend. When you hear that God is holy, remember He has been and always will be pure and holy. When you hear that God is faithful, remember He has the knowledge and power to fulfill all His promises. God is all these things forever. He will not change. As we piece these together, it helps us understand God's greatness and His perfection and that He is more than worthy of all praise and glory.

The question then becomes, *What do we do with this wonderful knowledge about God?* I would submit that it be used to develop a relationship with Him and to glorify Him.

God desires an intimate relationship with each one of us. One of the hallmarks of any close relationship is trust and love. With everything we know about God, He is worthy of our absolute trust. He loves you more than you can imagine. He knows every detail about you. He has an incredible plan for you and the power and knowledge to orchestrate it. He is with you every step of the way through the good and the bad.

In the midst of writing about trust, I was also reading through the book of Psalms. I came across Psalm 9:10's words, "Those who know your name trust in you, for you, Lord, have never forsaken those who seek you." It was not a coincidence that I came across this verse when I did. It is a joy to recognize these moments and feel His presence. Those who truly know I AM trust Him. How could we not trust Him?

As only God can do, He promises to bless us if we trust Him, "But I will bless the person who puts his trust in me. He is like a tree growing near a stream and sending out roots to the water. It is not afraid when hot weather comes, because its leaves stay green; it has no worries when there is no rain; it keeps on bearing fruit…" (Jeremiah 17:7-8, GNT).

When we truly trust God, we experience incredible freedom. Oftentimes we will put effort into something we hope to accomplish, and we will also pray about it. In trusting God, we should then release it and leave the outcome to Him. I believe it is freeing because we know that God wants only what is best for us. If it comes out the way we hope, of course, we are happy. If it does not come out the way we hope, we should still be content because we know that it is not in God's plan for us. Remember God's promise in Romans 8:28: "And we know that in all things God works for the good of those who love him, who have been called according to his purpose."

Along with trusting God, we are called to love Him. The Bible tells us that if we love God, we will obey Him. Jesus replied, "Anyone who loves me will obey my teaching" (John 14:23). Jesus gave us many teachings that we should obey, but I'd like to focus on the Great Commandment and the Great Commission.

The Great Commandment is to "Love the Lord your God with all your heart and with all your soul and with all your mind. This is the first and greatest commandment. And the second is like it: Love your neighbor as yourself. All the Law and the Prophets hang on these two commandments" (Matthew 22:37- 40). Sounds pretty simple, love God with everything you have in you and love others as you love yourself.

The Great Commission tells Christians to "…Go and make disciples of all nations, baptizing them in the name of the Father, the Son, and the Holy Spirit, and teaching them to obey everything I have commanded you" (Matthew 28:19–20). What does this look like practically? *The Purpose Driven Life* by Rick Warren practically breaks down what it means to live a life obedient to God, carrying out the Great Commandment and the Great Commission. It is one of the best-selling non-fiction books. The first sentence of the book says, "It's not about you."[1] Said another way, it is about God. The book goes through our five God-given purposes:

- Worship – We are called to worship God by surrendering to Him and trusting Him. Worship also includes growing our relationship with God by spending time with Him and spending time in His Word.

- Fellowship – We are called to live in Christian community via the church. The church is like a body, and we are part of that body. Without being connected to a church, we put ourselves at risk as we don't have access to the body of Christ, and we are shortchanging the body of Christ as it is missing a vital part (us!).

- Mature spiritually – We are called to become more like Christ, maturing and growing in our faith and knowledge.

- Ministry – We are called to serve God by finding our spiritual gifts and serving others.

- Mission – We are called to share the Gospel and carry out the Great Commission.

Our focus should be on God, His purposes for us, and on glorifying Him. If we do this, we get to live the most challenging, exciting, rewarding, impactful, and peace-filled life.

Some of you will read this and think that it would be dull to live a life obedient to God in large part because of the "shalt nots" contained in the Bible.

---

[1] Rick Warren, *The Purpose Driven Life* (Zondervan: 2002).

Knowing now what you know about God, you know that He is not punitive. He has given us these "shalt nots" for our own good. Remember, God only wants what is best for us. I like to think of the shalt nots as guard rails that God has given us to avoid the negative consequences of bad choices. In fact, God is a joyful god. Romans 15:13 states, "May the God of hope fill you with joy and peace as you trust in him, so that you may overflow with hope by the power of the Holy Spirit." God is able to fill us with joy because He is joyful. He is definitely *not* a killjoy.

Having said this, God's ways are not the ways of our culture or world. For example, it seems like today's culture is one of pride. We only have to look at our social media feeds for proof of this reality. Yet, God opposes the proud and gives grace to the humble (James 4:6).

Consider a wife's responsibility to submit to her husband (Ephesians 5:22). It seems like "submission" has become a dirty word. For a wife to submit to her husband in today's world is considered sexist by many. Unfortunately, what gets missed in this is a husband's responsibility to his wife. Ephesians 5:25 tells us that husbands are to *love their wives as Christ loves the church and gave himself up for her*. Please do not overlook this. Christ sacrificed himself for the church, and husbands are called to do the same for their wives. It's a bit of a rhetorical question, but wouldn't a wife want to submit to a husband that is so devoted to her that he would sacrifice himself for her? Knowing what we know about God, His ways have to be and are better than the world's.

As a dad, some of my prouder moments are when my son or daughter does something that I would do, or I'm told how much the kids are like me in some way. This makes me think about what God feels when others see Him in us. Wouldn't it be great for others to see our Father through us? I'd ask you to pause and ponder how it will feel when you see God in heaven for the first time. Can you imagine hearing the words "my son" or "my daughter" coming from Him with pride and love? And wouldn't it be awesome to have this followed up with "well done." Remember, *this is the God of the universe and our Abba Father all in one saying this.*

What steps can you take to hear these words?

Know that this incredible God, who loves you beyond belief, has a specific plan for your life. And since He is all-powerful, all-knowing, all-loving, never-changing, eternal, holy, and forever faithful, wouldn't His plan for you be better than your plan for you? It is not only the better plan, but the BEST plan for your life today into eternity!

The best life for you starts with stepping into a complete and selfless relationship with your heavenly Papa. He loves you. He is waiting to help you live your best life for Him. With this in mind, commit to God that you will spend the rest of your life seeking and living out God's plan for you, and then tell someone.

I AM is truly all you need.

Questions:

- Has your view of God changed? If so, how?
- What, if anything, are you going to do differently in your walk with God?
- Do you think a life lived pursuing God can be an exciting adventure?

The author is available for author interviews. For more information, contact us at info@advboooks.com

*A*dvantage
BOOKS

www.ingramcontent.com/pod-product-compliance
Lightning Source LLC
LaVergne TN
LVHW021525080426
835509LV00018B/2673